Young people and 'risk

Edited by Maggie Blyth, Enver Solomon and
Kerry Baker

**CENTRE FOR CRIME
AND JUSTICE STUDIES**

First published in Great Britain in 2007 by The Policy Press

The Policy Press
University of Bristol
Fourth Floor, Beacon House
Queen's Road
Bristol BS8 1QU
UK

Tel no +44 (0)117 331 4054
Fax no +44 (0)117 331 4093
E-mail tpp-info@bristol.ac.uk
www.policypress.org.uk

ISBN 978 1 84742 000 8

British Library Cataloguing in Publication Data
A catalogue record for this report is available from the British Library.

Library of Congress Cataloging-in-Publication Data
A catalog record for this report has been requested.

Cover image courtesy of iStockphoto®
Cover design by Qube Design Associates, Bristol
Printed in Great Britain by Latimer Trend, Plymouth

Contents

Preface

At the time of publication almost a decade will have passed since the youth justice reforms introduced a new statutory concept of multi-agency working with children and young people who offend. Working with new structures to oversee youth offending services at local level, the Youth Justice Board (YJB) has overseen policy and practice to monitor the youth justice system. During the same period, the National Offender Management Service (NOMS) has explored 'what works' in supervising young adults who offend. The next few months will see a period of even greater change with the new Ministry of Justice taking over all responsibility for offender management, criminal law and sentencing. For the youth justice system, it will be interesting to note how shared responsibility between the Ministry of Justice and the Department for Children, Schools and Families will impact on service delivery.

The preoccupation in working with adults who offend is now very much on public protection. For the youth justice system, the prevailing tone has continued to be on the prevention of youth crime and balancing meeting complex needs with managing risk. However, public and media pressure in the last two years has placed both systems in the political spotlight, with questions being asked about how effectively the risk presented by those who offend is managed. While NOMS has responded with a clear approach to risk management, there are still questions to be asked about appropriate strategies for work with young people. How should the wider issues of children's rights, safeguarding what is an extremely vulnerable group of individuals, and child protection be taken into account? What kind of assessment tools and models of engagement are most effective? Is public protection the most appropriate focus? How should prevention strategies be developed?

The intention behind this collection of papers is not necessarily to find the right answers to these questions but to contribute to a wider debate about the management and oversight of young people who commit serious crime. We hope that policy makers, managers in both criminal justice and children's services and others with an interest in children and young people who offend will all find something of value in the varied contributions and that the book will both challenge and stimulate their thinking.

Maggie Blyth
Enver Solomon
Kerry Baker

Acknowledgements

We would like to thank all those who took part in the seminar recorded through this publication and in particular Andrew Bridges, the Chief Inspector of Probation, for his introduction to the day. We are also grateful to the Youth Justice Board for England and Wales and the Parole Board for England and Wales for providing financial support to the seminar and to the Centre for Crime and Justice Studies for its help in organising the event.

Notes on contributors

Rob Allen is Director of the International Centre for Prison Studies at King's College London. He was previously Director of Rethinking Crime and Punishment at the Esmee Fairbairn Foundation in London, and, before that, Director of Research at the National Association for the Care and Resettlement of Offenders (NACRO) and Head of the Juvenile Offender Policy Unit in the UK Home Office. He was also a member of the Youth Justice Board for England and Wales for eight years. He has extensive experience of international penal reform work, mainly in the field of young people.

Sue Bailey, OBE, FRCPsych is Professor of Child and Adolescent Forensic Mental Health at the University of Central Lancashire.

Kerry Baker is a researcher at the Centre for Criminology at the University of Oxford and also a consultant to the Youth Justice Board on issues of assessment, risk and public protection. She has been closely involved in the development and validation of the Asset assessment profile currently used by all Youth Offending Teams (YOTs) in England and Wales. She has experience of working with both practitioners and policy makers in this field and has recently been responsible for developing guidance for youth justice staff on a range of public protection issues (such as MAPPA and 'dangerousness').

Maggie Blyth is former Head of Practice with the Youth Justice Board, where she oversaw national policy and practice issues for all YOTs. Prior to this she set up one of the first Youth Offending Services in 1999 following several years working as a senior manager within the Probation Service in Inner London and the Thames Valley. She is currently a member of the Parole Board for England and Wales and independent chair of Nottingham City YOT. She also works independently as a criminal justice consultant in the UK and Europe.

Gwyneth Boswell is Visiting Professor in the School of Allied Health Professions at the University of East Anglia (UEA) and Director of Boswell Research Fellows, an independent social research organisation. She is a former Senior Probation Officer and, for 15 years up to 2005, was closely involved in the training of probation officers at UEA and De Montfort University, where she was Professor of Criminology and Criminal Justice. She has researched widely into the backgrounds of young people who offend violently and the family ties of prisoners. She is the author of five books including *Young and dangerous* (1996), *Violent children and adolescents: Asking the question why* (2000) and *Imprisoned fathers and their children* with Peter Wedge (2002).

Ros Burnett is Senior Research Fellow at the Centre for Criminology, University of Oxford. Her research and teaching has centred on desistance from crime and the role of criminal justice agencies in assisting desistance. Her publications include: *Fitting supervision to offenders* (1996), *Joined-up youth justice* (with Catherine Appleton, 2003), *What works in probation and youth justice* (co-edited with Colin Roberts, 2004), and *Prisoners as citizens' advisers* (with Shadd Maruna, 2004). She is currently investigating the impact of the transition to the National Offender Management Service on frontline practice in probation and prisons.

Hazel Kemshall is currently Professor of Community and Criminal Justice at De Montfort University. Her research interests include the assessment and management of high-risk offenders, multi-agency public protection panels and community responses to sexual offenders. She has written extensively on risk, public protection and dangerousness, and has completed research for the Home Office, Scottish Executive and the ESRC.

Paul Mitchell is a mental health nurse who has worked in adolescent forensic psychiatry for many years in community, inpatient and custodial settings. He has developed and delivered cognitive behaviour therapy programmes to young people in custody and is currently completing his PhD looking at the factors affecting how young people in custody access mental health services.

Mike Nash is Head of Department and Deputy Director of the Institute of Criminal Justice Studies at the University of Portsmouth. He has worked at the University for 16 years and helped develop undergraduate programmes in criminology and criminal justice, community justice and police studies. Mike has researched and published widely in the field, especially in the area of dangerousness, producing his first book, *Police, probation and protecting the public* in 1999. He has a particular interest in the changing nature of the probation service and has recently written of its increasing association with the police service in the UK. He is presently co-writing a book on Serious Further Offences.

Enver Solomon is Deputy Director of the Centre for Crime and Justice Studies, an independent charity affiliated to the Law School at King's College London. He has previously worked as Head of Policy and Research at the Revolving Doors Agency, where he carried out an evaluation of the agency's link worker schemes with young people. Enver has also worked at the Prison Reform Trust, where he authored a report on young adults in custody. He has also published work on crime and the media and foreign national prisoners and recently co-authored a major analysis of the government's performance against key criminal justice targets, *Ten years of criminal* *justice under Labour: An independent audit* (2007). Prior to working on criminal justice policy he was a BBC journalist.

Robert Vermeiren is Professor of Child and Adolescent Psychiatry at the Leiden University Medical Center, Director of the child psychiatric clinic Curium, and Professor of Forensic Youth Psychiatry at the VU University Medical Center in Amsterdam, the Netherlands.

Introduction

Enver Solomon and Maggie Blyth

This book draws together the proceedings of a December 2006 seminar that examined a range of issues relating to young people and risk. The event was organised by the Centre for Crime and Justice Studies at King's College London with the Centre for Criminology, University of Oxford. It was funded and supported by the Youth Justice Board for England and Wales (YJB) and the Parole Board for England and Wales.

We decided to organise the seminar because there had been a number of high-profile cases that had focused widespread attention on the issue of risk and public protection.[1] The issue had not only assumed significant prominence within the criminal justice agenda but also in the wider politics of Westminster and was considered to be a key aspect in the failure of the Home Office, which was famously declared as 'dysfunctional' and 'unfit for purpose' by John Reid shortly after he became home secretary in May 2006.[2] Just two months later in July the Home Office published a wide-ranging review of criminal justice policy that set out new proposals for 'protecting the public from serious, violent and dangerous offenders' (Home Office, 2006b: 30). The review focused primarily on adults who offend but we took the view that the changing criminal justice policy landscape, increasingly centred on the concept of risk, was equally important for agencies working with children and young people under 18 years old.

Moreover, we were conscious that the Parole Board was being asked to consider the extent to which risk could be managed in the community in many cases of people who offend prolifically and persistently who had started offending under

---

[1] The case of John Monckton, murdered by two offenders, Damien Hanson and Elliot White, who were both under probation supervision in the community and the case of Anthony Rice, a sex offender on life licence in the community who murdered Naomi Bryant, both resulted in independent inquiries by the chief inspector of probation in 2006. They followed on from an inquiry into the case of Peter Williams in 2005, a young person convicted of murder while under statutory supervision by Nottingham YOT.

[2] Appearing before the Home Affairs Committee of the House of Commons on 23 May 2006, John Reid said that from 'time to time' the Home Office 'is dysfunctional', and he described the immigration and nationality director of the Home Office as 'not fit for purpose' (BBC News, 23 May 2006, available at: http://news.bbc.co.uk/1/hi/uk_politics/5007148.stm). This was subsequently quoted in the media and Parliament as referring to the entire Home Office department as being 'unfit for purpose'.

the age of 18. Indeed, the numbers of young people receiving new indeterminate sentences for public protection had doubled in the 12 months to December 2006 (Home Office, 2006a). Decisions on releasing these young people would rest entirely on an agreed understanding of risk assessment. It seemed to us that procedures underlying the risk management of young people who offend required urgent attention by policy makers and practitioners across the youth justice system. In particular, it was felt that for young people there are a range of different factors to consider both in relation to the organisational culture of youth justice services and in relation to adolescence itself which require policy makers to adopt alternative measures to those gaining dominance in the adult criminal justice system. The seminar was conceived to discuss these issues and to analyse critically the preoccupation with risk. This approach seemed to be of particular value given that, although the government was clearly determined to reform correctional services, the precise impact on children and young people in the youth justice system was less clear.

The seminar was held in London and participants included HM Chief Inspector of Probation, Andrew Bridges, and senior representatives from the YJB, the National Offender Management Service and the Parole Board. Academics, practitioners and representatives of the non-governmental organisations working in the criminal justice sector also attended.

We asked academic and practitioner experts in the field to prepare six papers to provide the basis of discussion at the event. This book includes revised versions of the papers together with an additional contribution from Ros Burnett looking at the substantial body of research into the early identification of risk factors associated with subsequent serious and persistent criminal behaviour.[3] This brief introduction and the conclusion by Rob Allen aim to capture the nature of the discussions and key themes that emerged at the seminar.

Clarifying terms: 'young people' and 'risk'

The focus of both the seminar and this book is on young people in the broadest sense of the term. We decided not to define an age band clearly but instead to focus both on children under the age of 18 and young adults into their early 20s. Although much of the focus is on children and young people in the youth justice system, we felt that the transition from childhood to adulthood is a gradual, developmental process that happens over the course of a number of years and that there were lessons for practitioners and policy makers working with young adults as well as those under the age of 18. In addressing the management of risk for

---

[3] It was decided to include this chapter at a later stage to ensure that all sides of the risk equation were covered in this volume.

this wider age range we hoped to emphasise that this transition is often slow and complex.

Having sought clarity on what we mean by young people it is equally important to set out what is meant by the notion of risk in relation to young people who offend. For the purposes of this book we have decided to look at the concept from three different perspectives. Firstly, there is the risk that young people who have been victims as well as perpetrators of crimes pose to themselves and how this may manifest itself in violent behaviour and different forms of mental health disorders. Secondly, there is the risk that young people who commit serious crimes pose to the public and how the agencies who work with them have developed assessment tools, procedures and practices to support them. To what extent has a new culture of public protection already taken hold and begun to affect working practices? Finally, there is the increased attention being given by government and policy makers to the early identification of children who exhibit risk factors that are thought to be linked to the likelihood of future serious offending and to indicate a need for preventive interventions.

Young people as victims and the risk they pose to themselves

Gwyneth Boswell's chapter (Chapter 3) considers the prevalence of abuse and loss in the childhoods of young people who offend violently. She emphasises the 'seemingly paradoxical but nevertheless close relationship between the young person's own victimisation at some point in their lives, and the offending'. This relationship exposes the vulnerability of children and young people who commit crime and how their own victimisation can result in their being just as much a danger to themselves as they are to others. Boswell argues that this is too often overlooked not only by the public but also by the criminal justice agencies.

In Chapter 4, Sue Bailey, Robert Vermeiren and Paul Mitchell explore in further detail the relationship between victimisation and violent offending among young people in the context of mental health disorders. They propose that young people and children who offend should be engaged by practitioners in a 'therapeutic alliance', and advocate 'listen[ing] attentively' and 'show[ing] interest in the young person's perspective' in order to establish 'the middle ground' within which such an alliance can be developed (p 64).

Many vulnerable children and young people respond to their experiences in the criminal justice system by either harming themselves or harming those around them. In Chapter 5, Maggie Blyth examines how the youth justice system deals with serious incidents and looks at what is known about the backgrounds of those young people who are involved in them. She concludes that there is a need for more detailed research and policy development to ensure that there is a greater understanding of the young people involved in serious incidents and more effective national oversight, management and accountability.

Young people and the risk they pose to others

Working with young people who have committed – or who may commit – serious crimes provides a range of challenges for practitioners. One of the most critical is ensuring that an effective assessment is carried out to identify the likelihood of future harm that the young person might pose to others. Based on research looking at data collated in the Asset assessment tool used by Youth Offending Teams (YOTs), and taking into account the limited work looking at the Offender Assessment System (OASys) assessment tool used by probation, Kerry Baker (Chapter 2) considers the knowledge and thinking processes used by practitioners to make complex judgements about risk. She argues that assessment tools could be improved to encourage practitioners to be more reflective and critical in their thinking and decision making. However, Baker cautions that changes to assessment tools can only go so far and that it is equally important to look at the impact of organisational cultures on how practitioners use and analyse information in making extremely difficult decisions.

Mike Nash (Chapter 6) considers whether or not the increasing preoccupation with public protection has resulted in a fundamental shift in the culture of criminal justice organisations. Is there now a specific, identifiable public protection culture that has come to dominate probation work and is it likely to be imposed on YOTs? Nash argues persuasively that probation and the National Offender Management Service within which it now sits has become much more of a corrections agency that is far removed from probation's welfarist roots. He concludes that the 'public protection culture is hugely influential and is undoubtedly becoming a defining ethos for the probation service' (p 92). For youth justice the cultural change is less advanced but nevertheless is equally pervasive. Nash is not confident that YOTs will be able to resist its advance into their territory.

However, Hazel Kemshall (Chapter 1) is in some ways more optimistic. She accepts that the 'adult risk prevention paradigm' has influenced youth justice but says 'an uncritical transition cannot be assumed' (p 17). According to Kemshall, there is now a greater focus in research, policy and practice on the social factors behind young people's offending and behaviour, which is having an impact on the assessment processes and responses that are adopted with young people. There is, therefore, the possibility of 'more balanced and holistic approaches to risk and youth than has been evidenced so far' (p 17).

Early risk factors and prevention

For the New Labour government, one of the key challenges facing criminal justice agencies and public services in general has been how to intervene early enough in the families of children who are likely to offend in the future. Risk prevention policies have also become increasingly popular not just for government but also among policy makers and social commentators. Several researchers have argued in favour of early interventions targeting at-risk infants and pre-school children to prevent the development of serious, chronic offending. It is clear that policy developments, such as the action plan to tackle social exclusion (Cabinet Office, 2006), have been influenced by research identifying early risk and protective factors as well as the long-term outcomes of some pre-school intervention programmes. The government seems intent on investing still further in targeted crime-prevention programmes, ensuring that YOTs and Children's Trusts work closely together. At the time of going to press a wide-ranging review on security, crime and justice proposed introducing universal checks throughout a child's development to identify those at risk of offending (Prime Minister's Strategy Unit, 2007). Ros Burnett (Chapter 7) provides a brief overview of some of this research to consider the empirical basis for such early intervention strategies and whether it is sufficiently robust for effective early assessment and targeting. She considers the practical and ethical implications of these early developmental prevention programmes and the related research.

Some of this is indeed controversial, especially that which implicates genetic variables and biological factors, while high-risk preventive strategies, which selectively target families and children considered to be most at risk, raise important questions about the accuracy of identification tools and stigmatising effects. But any consideration of the management of serious risk would be incomplete without discussion of this literature.

Burnett concludes that the literature is not as advanced as it could be but that, on balance, the early intervention agenda and policies should be pursued whilst the potential negative implications should not be overlooked.

Learning points for future practice

There are a number of key learning points for future practice raised by the contributions in this book. Firstly, and most importantly, is that although a focus on risk and public protection is important and sometimes necessary, it should be balanced with a requirement to focus on the safeguarding of children and young people. The current discourse around risky youth needs to be tempered with a greater recognition that young people who offend also remain children in need. At present there is a danger that policy and practice will drift down the same public protection road that has been taken for adults, without recognising that young people require a different, more balanced and less punitive approach.

Secondly, in establishing that risk management procedures do apply to young people as well as adults, it is imperative that policy and practice developments reflect the necessary differences outlined in the following chapters. Agencies such as the YJB need to develop a specialist approach to the assessment and management of risk of harm when working with young people, with supporting guidance provided to practitioners in the field. A new youth risk prevention paradigm should inform the risk assessments undertaken in wider National Offender Management Service work and, in particular, with the Parole Board. These new approaches need to be carefully constructed, be informed by a rights-based ethos and must take into account the vulnerabilities and complex needs of children and young people who offend.

Thirdly, to inform how best to extend the range of risk management approaches into work with children and young people who offend, a stronger and more wide-ranging evidence base must be encouraged. It is imperative that policy and practice are informed by such an evidence base rather than being pushed down politically imposed routes. This book is intended to assist with that process.

In conclusion, it seems clear to us that unless an exceptional case is made for the development of a specialist model for working with children and young people within the criminal justice arena – a model that is developed on the basis of the need paradigm rather than simply the risk paradigm – then both youth justice services and young adult teams are in danger of having to make use of existing, arguably more unsuitable risk management systems. There is a clear case to be made that the management of risk with children and young people who offend has distinctive qualities that are very different from mainstream practice with adults who offend and so require different models of working. We hope that the chapters in this book and the discussions at the preceding seminar will feed into the debate.

References

Cabinet Office (2006) *Reaching out: An action plan on social exclusion*, London: COI.

Home Office (2006a) *Population in custody. Monthly tables. December 2006*, London: Home Office.

Home Office (2006b) *Rebalancing the criminal justice system in favour of the law-abiding majority. Cutting crime, reducing reoffending and protecting the public*, London: Home Office.

Prime Minister's Strategy Unit (2007), *Policy review: Security, crime and justice*, London: Cabinet Office.

Risk assessment and risk management: the right approach?

Hazel Kemshall

Introduction and context

The 'risk business' has been described as one of the world's largest industries (Adams, 1995), characterised by phenomenal growth and net widening. Crime management has been no exception, with risk forming a key ingredient of penal policy in recent years (see Kemshall, 2003 and 2006 for a full review). In the adult arena this has seen increased attention to the 'community protection model' (Connelly and Williamson, 2000), with an emphasis upon public protection sentencing, restrictive conditions in the community, and interventions led by risk (Wood and Kemshall, 2007). Within this paradigm, adults who offend have largely been characterised as 'risk taking', intransigent, morally unworthy, and in need of corrective treatment, moral re-education and 'responsibilisation' (see Kemshall, 2002a for a further discussion). Where such moral re-engineering programmes fail, monitoring, surveillance and 'management in place' are justified (Feeley and Simon, 1994; Garland, 1996, 1997 and 2001; O'Malley, 2004 and 2006). This has resulted in a peculiar bifurcation in the management of risk, with those deemed amenable to change subject to risk management strategies based on behaviour change and cognitive treatments; and those deemed intransigent or non-compliant subject to risk management strategies based on containment and exclusion. While there have often been difficulties in operating such bifurcation in a pure form (Kemshall, 2002a), it is possible to discern such tactics in the operation of the multi-agency public protection arrangements (MAPPA) and in the community management of those who offend who pose a high risk (Kemshall, 2003). The community protection model has also been given added impetus by high-profile risk management failures (in both the adult and youth justice arenas), and by intensive media coverage of both systemic and individual failures (Thomas, 2005).

The pervasiveness of risk has seeped into the youth justice arena and more broadly into social policy conceptions and responses to youth (Kemshall, 2007), resulting in an increased 'problematisation of youth' (Kelly, 2000) and state-driven interventions (predominantly through criminal justice agencies) to regulate and control youth. It is, however, tempting to make grand claims about the ubiquitous nature of risk, particularly at the policy level, although such claims can often be difficult to evidence empirically (Dingwall, 1999; Kemshall and Maguire, 2001; O'Malley, 2004). As Kelly argues, young people have long occupied the 'wild zones' of 'deviancy', 'delinquency', and 'ungovernability', but the key difference now is the 'institutionalised mistrust' of youth, all youth (2003, 2006).

Within this context, dealing with 'troubled' or 'troublesome' young people is now a major policy concern (Goldson, 2000; Case, 2006). Indeed, identifying 'at-risk' youth has spawned an industry, with Swadner and Lubeck (1995) arguing that in the United States between 1989 and 1995 over 2,500 articles on at-risk children and families were published (see also Tait, 1995 for the framing of the 'at-risk' discourse; and Muncie, 2005, on the globalisation of crime control and implications for youth justice). Policies and interventions also proliferated in the 1990s, ranging (in the UK) from early interventions (Farrington, 1995) including Sure Start (Glass, 1999), assessing children in need (*Every Child Matters*, DfES, 2003), those in danger of a 'mis-spent youth' (Audit Commission, 1996; Audit Scotland, 2002), and those at risk of developing a criminal career (Farrington, 2000). For some commentators, (most notably Tait, 1995; Goldson, 1999, 2000 and 2002; Kelly, 2003; Whyte, 2003; Sharland, 2006), the 'problematising of youth' has resulted in a blurring of social policy and crime policy in which social problems are reframed as crime problems and crime-control strategies are increasingly deployed to manage intractable social ills. This has been particularly prevalent in responses to marginalised and excluded communities (Yates, 2004 and 2006), and the failure to regulate youth effectively through the labour market (Jordan, 2000). For Muncie, this has resulted in an 'institutionalised intolerance' of youth (1999) and an over-regulation of youth (see for example Smith, 2003 and 2006).

This institutionalised intolerance has resulted in a 'punitive populist' response to youth crime, with a doubling of custodial sentences since 1992 in a decade that has seen youth crime decrease by 16% (Nacro, 2003 and 2005). The United Nations Commissioner on Human Rights noted that 'juvenile troublemakers' in the UK were 'too rapidly drawn into the criminal justice system and young offenders are too readily placed in detention' (Gil-Robles, 2005: 27). The United Kingdom currently has one of the highest juvenile prison populations in Western Europe (Goldson, 2005). This is against a backdrop of falling crime rates but heightened public, media and political perceptions to the contrary (Pitts, 2000 and 2003; Tonry, 2004). The increased regulation and surveillance of young people, particularly in public spaces, and the increased use of intensive supervision (for example ISSP [Intensive Supervision and Surveillance Programme]) has also raised concerns, not least from the head of the Youth Justice Board (YJB) (Morgan, 2006). Such intensive intervention programmes have not reduced the use of custody, and in some instances their breach rate has resulted in faster routes to custody for young people (Morgan, 2006). Arguably, such over-regulation (and particularly the overuse of custody) erodes the rights of young people and prevents their passage into the much desired 'active citizenship' (Goldson, 2002; Kelly, 2003).

Set against this trend is the increased attention by social commentators and social policy makers to the marginalisation, exclusion and vulnerability of young people, particularly as they navigate the life course and key transitions from youth to adulthood (Evans, 2002). Central to this position has been the early identification of 'problematic' children and families for early interventions, and programmes targeted at the alleviation of risk factors at particular points during the life course, for example Sure Start, literacy programmes, school inclusion projects, and assistance in the transition from school to work, such as Connexions (Glass, 1999; Schoon and Bynner, 2003). Fundamental to this approach is the identification of risk factors and risk trajectories in which one risk factor 'reinforces another, leading to increasingly restricted outcomes in later life (Rutter, 1990)' (Schoon and Bynner, 2003: 23). While the ensuing interventions are often presented in the discourse of care, protection and support (DoH and DfEE, 2000; Garrett, 2003), ensuring social cohesion and economic performance are also key considerations (Kelly, 2006). The costs of not pursuing policies are also pertinent, for example in the costs of social exclusion (Social Exclusion Unit, 2000a and 2000b), the perpetuation of a dependent (and potentially criminal) underclass (Murray, 1990) and the social dislocation of 'sink estates' (Campbell, 1993).

These risk prevention policies have the following in common:

- a focus on the individual and family as the site of risk and regulation;
- a formal, calculable and probabilistic approach to risk.

While families and individuals have long been the site of social engineering and social regulation, not least through the 'soft policing' of the welfare state, education and the informal controls of the labour market (Donzelot, 1980), in recent decades increasing attention has focused on 'breaking the cycle of dependence' and dysfunction, and in the alleviation of accumulated risk factors through the life course (Schoon and Bynner, 2003). This has been particularly acute under New Labour, with its emphasis upon 'rights as well as responsibilities' (Blair, 1998) and the alleviation of inequality through the labour market rather than through welfare (see Kemshall, 2002b for a full review). The contrast between these two 'contexts' can often be stark (although they also elide), and the tension between them is regularly played out in both policy and practice, for example in:

- risks versus needs (Boswell, 1997 and 1999);
- the content and structure of risk tools, and indeed how they are received and used by staff (Baker, Chapter 2 in this volume);
- the conflation of vulnerability and risk;
- risk of reoffending with the risk of harm;
- risks versus rights – and the extent to which rights for young people should be conditional on their law-abiding compliance and lack of risk.

The policy and practice debate about whether we are responding to 'children in need' or 'risky youth' has been fierce (see Goldson, 2000 and 2002 for a full review). Policy and practice change under New Labour has in effect seen a blurring of this distinction. For example, while interventions are often expressed in the language of care, protection and support (DoH and DfEE, 2000; Garrett, 2003), ensuring social integration and positive transition into the labour force are also key considerations (Kelly, 2006). The language of 'need', 'at risk' and vulnerability has begun to elide into the language of risk, harm and danger. *Every Child Matters* (DfEE, 2003) and the 2004 Children Act, extend concerns and interventions to children not only in need of protection but also to children seen as presenting a risk to others (Sharland, 2006). The Youth Inclusion Projects targeted at the 50 most troubled children in the community also characterise such children as the most troublesome. In essence, early prevention is targeted at 'needs' but justified on the basis of preventing future risks, and most particularly the risk of crime.

The tension between needs and risks is also played out in risk tools, with some tools such as Asset attempting to capture both vulnerability and risk, and re-characterising some needs (such as accommodation) as risk factors through the emphasis upon 'criminogenic need', that is, needs that are legitimate for attention because they are correlated with offending (Kemshall, 2003). The coverage of the tools, and often their emphasis upon risk, prevention and control, has affected the commitment of workers to their use (see Baker, Chapter 2 in this volume). At its most acute, this can be expressed as an ideological clash between workers who wish to focus on vulnerability, and policy makers who wish to focus on public protection (Kemshall, 2007). The conflation of the risk of reoffending with the risk of harm has also exacerbated the tension between needs and risks. Instances of high harm offences (for example, the murder of Jamie Bulger) heighten anxieties about youth crime out of proportion to its actual prevalence (Goldson, 1999), and conversely the perceived prevalence of low-level crimes with a high impact on quality of life (and those crimes are often prey to extensive media coverage) can heighten perceptions of risk (Muncie, 1999 and 2006).

The risk agenda has also tended to prioritise public protection and diminish the rights of children and young people. Scraton and Haydon (2002: 313) contrast the limitations of children's rights and their experience of harm – such as abuse, trafficking and exploitation – with the rights and safety enjoyed by adults (Children's Rights Office, 1995; Howard League for Penal Reform, 2005: 8). The imbalance between the harms children pose to society and the social harms they are exposed to has been the subject of increasing comment (see Hillyard et al, 2005). Within current policy, rights, even for children, are conditional with 'no rights without responsibilities' (Blair, 1998), and the 'new youth justice' emphasises responsibilities *and* rights (Muncie, 2004). Those who are deemed 'irresponsible' because they commit crime, or who fail to take on the responsibilities of education, training or employment, are deemed to have fewer rights. For them, greater levels of intrusion and regulation are justified.

Risk assessment: the right approach?

The emphasis upon criminal careers gained ground in the 1980s under New Right governments in most anglophone countries concerned with the burgeoning costs of custody and the failure to deter those who offend persistently (Blumstein et al, 1986). According to Farrington, this fostered an interest in risk and protective factors that could influence both the development and targeting of intervention programmes (2000), particularly in the face of rising youth crime and a need to demonstrate value for money.

The growing policy preoccupation with risky youth and 'at-risk' youth has resulted in increased attention to 'developmental careers' (Loeber and Le Blanc, 1990) and the formation of 'interventions designed to prevent the development of criminal potential in individuals' (Farrington, 2000: 3). This approach is attractive because it promises a more effective focus for policy and better targeting of programmes and practitioner resources. Characterised as the 'risk prevention paradigm' (Farrington, 2000: 1), this approach emphasises risk prediction and early identification. As Armstrong (2004) has pointed out, this approach has been central to the UK's youth crime reduction approach (Youth Justice Board, 2001), with some variability in Scotland (Whyte, 2003). The paradigm is dependent upon profiling individuals against risk factors generated by research and applied through the use of formal risk assessment tools such as Asset (Youth Justice Board, 2001), resulting in what some have described as a 'risk factorology' approach to risk assessment (Kemshall, 2003). This approach has also extended to 'communities at risk' (Hawkins and Catalano, 1992; Catalano and Hawkins, 1996) that are prey to antisocial behaviour, crime, disadvantage and social exclusion (Social Exclusion Unit, 2000a and 2000b).

Do risk factors help us?

However, risk prediction remains difficult, with the linkage of a risk factor(s) to a criminal pathway(s) proving to be particularly problematic (Farrington, 2000). This is due in large part to the difficulty in establishing the relationship between a risk factor(s) and subsequent offending; in essence, demonstrating causal relationships and establishing the relative causal weight of differing risk factors. The issue is well expressed by Farrington, who asks how we distinguish between causal relationships and mere correlations, how we can attribute weight to different factors when causes may be multifactoral, and how levels of risk can be calculated when risk 'scores' are not merely additive (Farrington, 2000: 7).

For Farrington, the greater challenge is in establishing 'processes or developmental pathways that intervene between risk factors and outcomes, and to bridge the gap between risk factor research and more complex explanatory theories'

(2000: 7). This may require the recognition that pathways are social processes that have multiple causes, and that such causes are not merely additive, and that subtle differences in initial conditions may, over time, produce large differences in outcomes (Byrne, 1998: 2–28). This would help to explain why children who are initially similarly risk-marked (for example, by individual and family risk markers) actually go on to have different crime pathways, and why a proportion of children marked as 'high risk' for later delinquency do not offend. The statistical modelling and meta-analyses of this approach have not been able to explain why the individualised risk factor approach cannot predict the career paths of the majority of young people who offend, and why predetermined pathways have not always turned out to be that determined. In essence, this is the perennial tension between the 'rates question' – the extent to which a behaviour occurs in the population as a whole – and the 'conduct question', that is, why particular individuals do what they do (Leavitt, 1999).

Meta-analytical investigations of risk factors tend to deal with the 'rates question', whereas risk assessment tools like Asset tend to deal with the 'conduct question', although their content is derived from the rates question. Practitioners are tasked with answering and managing the conduct question, but often use techniques and tools derived from the rates-question approach to do it. Unsurprisingly, they experience numerous tensions as they do so (see Baker, Chapter 2 in this volume).

While the risk prevention paradigm has contributed much to policy and practice (Farrington, 1995 and 2000), not least various risk assessment tools such as Asset, the Structured Assessment of Violence Risk in Youth (SAVRY) (Borum et al, 2006), the risk prevention paradigm has been criticised on a number of grounds. In particular, risk-led policy strategies can be difficult to implement in practice, not least because risk categories can be difficult to define and difficult to operate in practice (Kemshall et al, 2005). Such categorisations require accurate and reliable assessment tools and that these tools are used with inter-rater reliability, requirements that cannot always be met (see Baker, Chapter 2 in this volume). The preventative paradigm has also been criticised for failing to give 'voice' to young people and for reflecting governmental strategies to control and regulate youth rather than to include and promote their concerns (Armstrong, 2004; France, 2006). In essence, this results in imposed risks rather than in youth-generated needs. Such risk factors have also been critiqued for their limited nature (largely generated from studies of white males) (Hansen and Plewis, 2004; Case, 2006).

Risk taking for young people has been seen as increasingly more complex with increased attention to social context, social processes and the interaction between individual agency and social structure becoming more important (Kemshall et al, 2006). Deployment of individual agency in risk decision making has attracted much research interest, with attention to how risks are negotiated, how choices are constrained, and the context within which decisions are made (Rhodes, 1997).

Research in this area focuses on contextual and structural issues and casts the rational actor as a *social* actor, and the focus is upon how these processes work and impact upon risk decisions. Research on juvenile crime has focused increasingly on the process of risk decision making, the influence of immediate context, and interaction with significant others as such decisions are made (see the work of Wikström, 2002, 2004a and 2004b). For Wikström the 'perception of alternatives and the process of choice' is itself key (2004a: 7). Risk decisions are the outcome of such choices and of how individuals interact with their immediate locales. This approach begins to explain why children with similar risk markers can make significantly different risk decisions. It only requires one or two small factors to be different for a large difference in a crime pathway to result.

Increased attention to social context has focused attention on social factors like housing, employment and positive social networks (May, 1999; Farrall, 2002). These factors have a role in producing social investment and stability for many young people who offend (Sampson and Laub, 1993; Laub and Sampson, 2001), although their exact weight in desistance from crime and how they interact is a matter of some debate (May, 1999). More recently the role of social structure in desistance has been extended beyond social factors to include notions of power, opportunity and constraint – for example, the structure of employment opportunities, access and use of social networks, and the range and type of 'social capital' available to young people (Farrall, 2002; Kemshall et al, 2003; Bottoms et al, 2004). This is not merely about the young person's capacity to make informed choices, it is about the structure of opportunity itself and the range of choices genuinely available (Wright Mills, 1970).

In this approach, negotiating risks is seen as dependent upon individual agency, constraint and opportunity, contingency and context, power and cultural/structural processes. This approach is, however, relatively new and is only just beginning to build up a body of empirical knowledge. With the exception of Farrall and Bowling (1999), Maruna (2001) and Bottoms et al (2004), the approach is also relatively under-theorised although it is utilising a large body of sociological theory. It gives a 'voice' and importance to young people's own accounts (France, 2000). However, there is some dispute about the status of such accounts and whether they become retrospective justifications for actions and choices (Bottoms et al, 2004). Prospective research may counteract this (Bottoms et al, 2004), although these studies may encounter problems of sample attrition as participants leave or are incarcerated.

Risk management: the right approach?

While there has been some importation of adult risk management strategies to work with young people, it is increasingly recognised that young people should not be treated as the passive recipients of adult-based interventions. The following key principles are suggested to inform risk management with young people:

- Risk management should be just, proportionate and fair, and targeted at well-assessed risk factors.
- Interventions should have regard to levels of maturity, learning capacity and the social skill level of children and adolescents.[1]
- Cognitive behavioural programmes should be age appropriate, sensitive to the learning style of the young person and supported by appropriate motivational work and reinforcement.
- A traditional learning style is likely to be inappropriate for many young offenders, as many of them will have had unsatisfactory experiences in school.

Many young people who offend have particular barriers to learning that may affect their ability to engage in cognitive behavioural or other programmes. Practitioners should ensure that information from Asset and other relevant sources is used to establish barriers to such learning (for example, literacy levels) and the preferred learning style of the young person.

Managing the risk of harm (as distinct from the risk of reoffending) presents other key issues, not least acting in a manner proportionate to the risks posed. The key principle is that restrictive conditions and levels of intrusion should be both necessary and in proportion to the risk of harm posed (Home Office, 2004). This requires a careful and accountable balancing of the rights of the individual (for example to privacy) against the rights of the public to protection (see Kemshall and Wood [forthcoming] for a full review). It is important that young people do not see such restrictive conditions (exclusion zones, curfews, tagging, tracking) as overly intrusive and 'unfair', as these perceptions can have an impact upon compliance (Wood and Kemshall, 2007). Where such conditions are fully explained, seen as justified or as 'common sense', they are accepted and more often complied with (Wood and Kemshall, 2007). The combination of public protection measures (such as restrictive conditions and monitoring) with rehabilitative and reintegrative measures are seen as having the best impact (Kemshall et al, 2005; Wood and Kemshall, 2007). For example, supervision packages that combine limited and controlled disclosure to teaching staff can enable a young person who offends sexually to return to college, facilitating both public protection and reintegration. It is also important that group-based treatment and intervention programmes are supported by specifically tailored one-to-one work and emphasis upon relapse prevention. In addition, there is growing evidence that children and young

---

[1] The Department of Health and the Dartington Research Unit have provided a maturation guide used in the assessment of 'looked-after children', which takes account of: health, education, identity, relationships, social presentation, emotional and behavioural development and self-care skills (DoH and DfEE, 2000).

people who commit 'grave crimes'[2] (for example, murder, attempted murder, manslaughter) have experienced sexual abuse, physical abuse, significant family stressors (for example, witnessing family violence), or traumatic life experiences such as loss of a parent (Bailey, 1996; Boswell, 1997, 1999 and Chapter 3 in this volume), although it must be stressed that not all children who experience abuse and loss will offend violently.

Other useful risk management tactics are:

- stable and suitable accommodation;
- positive involvement of parents, carers and mentors;
- specific therapies (for example on sexual offending);
- addressing drug, substance and alcohol abuse;
- constructive use of leisure time;
- avoidance of antisocial peers;
- school attendance;
- employment (see Youth Justice Board, 2001 and 2005).

In addition, recent work has emphasised the building of positive support networks for young people and enabling them to access a wider structure of opportunity (Boeck et al, 2006). Such networks can enhance the radius of trust young people have, and enable the development of more positive relationships with adults. Pro-social involvement and attachment to pro-social adult role models have also been positively evaluated for violence risk reduction (Hoge et al, 1996; Caprara et al, 2001). This work has been supported by an increased focus on protective factors and resilience. The following protective factors have been seen as particularly important for the reduction of violent behaviour:

- Pro-social involvement with pro-social peers and adults. This includes the pursuit of pro-social activities such as organised sports, leisure clubs, etc. It can include positive role modelling to assist children in developing coping strategies to resist aggressive behaviours, particularly when stressed (Borum et al, 2006).
- Encouragement and reinforcement of pro-social behaviours. As Caprara et al express it: 'Pro-social behaviour can also be a powerful antidote to aggression when earlier emotional vulnerability and negative interpersonal experiences, through rejection and stigmatization, lead to hostility, disengagement, and social withdrawal' (2001: 201). In essence, this reduces social isolation and creates a buffer to further criminality (Borum et al, 2006).

---

[2] For example, those crimes committed by an offender aged between 10 and 17 which, if committed by an adult, would be punishable by 14 years or more, section 53 of the 1933 Children and Young Persons Act, and section 91 of the 2000 Powers of Criminal Courts (Sentencing) Act, section 90 PCC(S) 2000, section 61 of the 2000 Criminal Justice and Courts Act.

• Creation and maintenance of strong social bonds, particularly to pro-social adults, can mitigate against future violence, particularly relationships that are both positive and validate the young person's ability to avoid offending.

A positive attitude towards 'authority' and interventions is also mentioned by Borum et al as a protective factor, as is school inclusion. However, some young people will have had a cumulative, negative experience of authority over their childhood (including breaches of trust and a sense of being 'let down'). In these circumstances, establishing trust may be a prerequisite of rebuilding cooperation with, and respect for, authority. School inclusion has been similarly promoted as a key to anti-criminal behaviour. However, more recent studies have also noted that schools can be places of fear, stress and difficulty for some children, and that forced inclusion can be counterproductive. Alternative educational measures are sometimes a route to more productive risk management (see Kemshall et al, 2006).

Promoting resilience to crime, and especially to violent crime, has also proved problematic. Garmezy (1993) has described resilience as a rich mixture of factors inherent to the individual child, factors in their immediate environment, and sources of support available to them. In essence, risk protection is seen as a process, and resilience as a personal product of the individual, generated and supported by positive networks such as parenting programmes and school inclusion. However, how these factors actually interact has proved difficult to discern (Kemshall et al, 2006), and hence this makes translation into effective programmes more difficult. Some children prove to be remarkably resilient and respond well, and others do not, although their risk markers may be very similar. This makes a 'one size fits all' approach to programmes to promote resilience difficult; highly individualised approaches are likely to have more impact.

Case management and the effective delivery of risk management are also significant. The following have been seen as critical for the management of high-risk cases: consistency of worker(s); clear procedures and adherence to agency policies; rapid response including rapid enforcement in the face of low compliance and escalating risk; combined methods; and contingency plans in case of breakdown or significant changes in circumstances (Kemshall and Maguire, 2001; see also Lipsey and Wilson, 1999). Effective risk management within custodial settings requires a combination of effective programmes, pro-social modelling by staff, pastoral care, and positive regimes (Dale et al, 1999; Richards and Smith, 2000). Risk management plans should clearly indicate how risky behaviours will be addressed during the custodial period (there is a tendency to focus on immediate risk management issues within the secure environment at the expense of longer-term issues).

Institutional programmes focused on interpersonal skills and using cognitive behavioural therapy techniques are the most effective for the reduction of aggressive behaviour (Lipsey and Wilson, 1993). Programmes using a multidisciplinary approach to risk management with attention to offending behaviour, anger management and pre-release work are the most effective. Planning points of transition within the sentence through differing parts of the secure estate and into the adult prison system are particularly beneficial, combined with regular reviews targeting the needs and risks of the young person. Early planning for release, including, where appropriate, referral to MAPPA, also contributes to effective risk management (Kemshall et al, 2005).

Conclusion

The adult risk prevention paradigm has spread into the youth justice arena, and while some positive contribution can be discerned (for example, in some of the structured risk assessment tools and effective programmes), an uncritical transition cannot be assumed. Young people are significantly different, and both risk assessment and risk management must take these differences into consideration. The current policy and media characterisations of youth 'at risk' and 'posing a risk' are also significant here, and both the 'problematisation of youth' and 'institutional intolerance' of youth have been major drivers in the risk agenda with youth. This has resulted in policies that reflect a more punitive, controlling and regulatory function than policies that are enabling, focused on context and opportunity and attempt to create positive networks of support and choice. More recent attention in research, policy and practice to social factors, social context and structural issues is extending the remit of risk assessment and also extending the range of risk management responses adopted with young people. This may offer the chance for more balanced and holistic approaches to risk and youth than has been evidenced so far.

References
Adams, J. (1995) *Risk*, London: UCL Press.
Armstrong, D. (2004) 'A risky business? Research, policy and governmentality and youth offending', *Youth Justice*, vol 4, no 2, pp 100–16.
Audit Commission (1996) *Mis-spent youth*, London: Audit Commission.
Audit Scotland (2002) *Dealing with offending by young people*, Edinburgh: Audit Scotland.
Bailey, S. (1996) 'Adolescents who murder', *Journal of Adolescence*, vol 19, no 1, pp 19–39.
Blair, T. (1998) *The Third Way*, London: The Fabian Society.
Blumstein, A., Cohen, J., Roth, J.A. and Visher, C.A. (1986) (eds), *Criminal careers and 'career criminals'*, Washington, DC: National Academy Press.
Boeck, T., Fleming, J. and Kemshall, H. (2006) 'The context of risk decisions: Does social capital make a difference?', *Forum Qualitative Research*, vol 7, no 1, art. 17, January (available at: www/qualitative-research.net/fqs-texte/1-06/06-1-17-e.htm, accessed 24 October 2006).
Borum, R., Bartel, P. and Forth, A. (2006) 'Manual for the structured assessment of violence risk in youth', Version 1, Florida: University of South Florida.

Boswell, G. (1997) 'The backgrounds of violent young offenders: The present picture', in V. Varma (ed), *Violence in children and adolescents*, London: Jessica Kingsley Publishers, pp 22–36.

Boswell, G. (1999) 'Young offenders who commit grave crimes: The criminal justice response', in H. Kemshall and J. Pritchard (eds), *Good practice in working with violence*, London: Jessica Kingsley Publishers, pp 33–49.

Bottoms, A., Shapland, J., Costello, A., Holmes, D. and Muir, G. (2004) 'Towards desistance: Theoretical underpinnings for an empirical study', *Howard Journal of Criminal Justice*, vol 43, no 3, pp 338–68.

Byrne, D. (1998) *Complexity theory and the social science*, London: Routledge.

Campbell, B. (1993) *Goliath: Britain's dangerous places*, London: Methuen.

Caprara, G., Barbaranelli, C. and Pastorelli, C. (2001) 'Prosocial behaviour and aggression in childhood and pre-adolescence', in A. Bohart and D. Stipek (eds), *Constructive and destructive behaviour: Implications for family, school and society*, Washington, DC: American Psychological Association, pp 187–203.

Case, S. (2006) 'Young people "at risk" of what? Challenging risk-focused early interventions as crime prevention', *Youth Justice*, vol 6, no 3, pp 171–9.

Catalano, R.F. and Hawkins, J.D. (1996) 'The social development model: A theory of anti-social behaviour', in J. Hawkins (ed), *Delinquency and crime: Current theories*, Cambridge: Cambridge University Press, pp 149–98.

Children's Rights Office (1995) *Making the convention work for children*, London: Children's Rights Office.

Connelly, C. and Williamson, S. (2000) *Review of the research literature on serious violent and sexual offenders*, Crime and Criminal Justice Research Findings no 46, Edinburgh: Scottish Executive Central Research Unit.

Dale, C., Allan, G. and Brennan, W. (1999) 'Violence in high secure hospital settings', in H. Kemshall and J. Pritchard (eds), *Good practice in working with violence*, London: Jessica Kingsley Publishers, pp 207–30.

Department for Education and Skills (2003) *Every Child Matters*, Green Paper, London: Department for Education and Skills (available at: www.dfes.gov.uk/everychildmatters).

Department of Health and Department for Education and Employment, Home Office (2000) *Framework for the assessment of children in need and their families*, London: The Stationery Office.

Dingwall, R. (1999) '"Risk society": The cult of theory and the millennium?', *Social Policy and Administration*, vol 33, no 4, pp 474–91.

Donzelot, J. (1980) *The policing of families*, London: Hutchinson.

Evans, K. (2002) 'Taking control of their lives? Agency in young adult transitions in England and the New Germany', *Journal of Youth Studies*, vol 5, no 3, pp 245–69.

Farrall, S. (2002) *Rethinking what works with offenders: Probation, social context, and desistance from crime*, Cullompton: Willan.

Farrall, S. and Bowling, B. (1999) 'Structuration, human development and desistance from crime', *British Journal of Criminology*, vol 39, no 2, pp 252–67.

Farrington, D.P. (1995) 'The development of offending and antisocial behaviour from childhood: Key findings from the Cambridge study in delinquent development', *Journal of Child Psychology and Psychiatry*, vol 36, no 6, pp 929–64.

Farrington, D.P. (2000) 'Explaining and preventing crime: The globalization of knowledge – The American Society of Criminology 1999 presidential address', *Criminology*, vol 38, no 1, pp 1–24.

Feeley, M. and Simon, J. (1994) 'Actuarial justice: The emerging new penal law', in D. Nelken (ed), *The futures of criminology*, London: Sage Publications, pp 173-201.

France, A. (2000) 'Towards a sociological understanding of youth and their risk taking', *Journal of Youth Studies*, vol 3, no 3, pp 317–31.

France, A. (2006) *Youth in late modernity*, Milton Keyes: Open University Press.

Garland, D. (1996) 'The limits of the sovereign state: Strategies of crime control in contemporary society', *British Journal of Criminology*, vol 36, no 4, pp 445–71.

Garland, D. (1997) '"Governmentality" and the problem of crime: Foucault, criminology and sociology', *Theoretical Criminology*, vol 1, no 2, pp 164–73.

Garland, D. (2001) *The culture of crime control: Crime and social order in contemporary society*, Oxford: Oxford University Press.

Garmezy, N. (1993) 'Vulnerability and resilience', in D. Funder and R. Parke (eds), *Studying lives through time: Personality and development*, Washington, DC: American Psychological Association, pp 377–98.

Garrett, P.M. (2003) 'Swimming with dolphins: The assessment framework, new Labour and new tools for social work with children and families', *British Journal of Social Work*, vol 33, no 4, pp 441–63.

Gil-Robles, A. (2005) *Report by the Commissioner for Human Rights on his visit to the United Kingdom*, Strasbourg: Office of the Commissioner for Human Rights.

Glass, N. (1999) 'Sure Start: The development of an early intervention programme for young children in the United Kingdom', *Children and Society*, vol 13, no 4, pp 257–64.

Goldson, B. (1999) 'Youth (in)justice: Contemporary developments in policy and practice', in B. Goldson (ed) *Youth justice: Contemporary policy and practice*, Aldershot: Ashgate.

Goldson, G. (2000) '"Children in need" or "young offenders"? Hardening ideology, organizational change and new challenges for social work with children in trouble', *Child and Family Social Work*, vol 5, no 3, pp 255–65.

Goldson, G. (2002) 'New Labour, social justice and children: Political calculation and the deserving-undeserving schism', *British Journal of Social Work*, vol 32, no 6, pp 683–95.

Goldson, G. (2005) 'Taking liberties: Policy and the punitive turn', in H. Hendrick (ed) *Child welfare and social policy: An essential reader*, Bristol: The Policy Press, pp 255-67.

Hansen, J. and Plewis, I. (2004) *Children at risk: How evidence from British cohort data can inform the debate on prevention*, London: University of London.

Hawkins, D.J. and Catalano, R.F. (1992) *Communities that care*, San Francisco: Jossey-Bass.

Hillyard, P., Polantzis, C., Tombs, S., Gordon, D. and Dorling, D. (2005) (eds), *Criminal obsessions: Why harm matters more than crime*, London: Crime and Society Foundation.

Hoge, R., Andrews, D. and Leschied, A. (1996) 'An investigation of risk and protective factors in a sample of youthful offenders', *Journal of Child Psychology and Psychiatry and Allied Disciplines*, vol 37, no 4, pp 419–24.

Home Office (2004) *MAPPA guidance version 2*, London: Home Office.

Howard League for Penal Reform (2005) *Children in custody: Promoting the legal and human rights of children*, London: The Howard League for Penal Reform.

Jordan, B. (2000) *Social work and the third way: Tough love as social policy*, London: Sage Publications.

Kelly, P. (2000) 'Youth as an artefact of expertise: Problematising the practice of youth studies', *Journal of Youth Studies*, vol 3, no 3, pp 301–15.

Kelly, P. (2003) 'Growing up as risky business? Risks, surveillance and the institutionalised mistrust of youth', *Journal of Youth Studies*, vol 6, no 2, pp 165–80.

Kelly, P. (2006) 'The entrepreneurial self and "youth at risk": Exploring the horizons of identity in the twenty-first century', *Journal of Youth Studies*, vol 9, no 1, pp 17–32.

Kemshall, H. (2002a) 'Effective practice in probation: An example of "advanced liberal responsibilisation"', *Howard Journal of Criminal Justice*, vol 41, no 1, pp 41–58.

Kemshall, H. (2002b) *Risk, social policy and welfare*, Buckingham: Open University Press.

Kemshall, H. (2003) *Understanding risk in criminal justice*, Buckingham: Open University Press.

Kemshall, H. (2006) 'Crime and risk', in P. Taylor-Gooby and J. Zinn (eds), *Risk in social science*, Oxford: Oxford University Press, pp 76–93.

Kemshall, H. (2007) 'Risk, social policy and young people', in J. Wood and J. Hine (eds), *Work with young people: Developments in theory, policy and practice*, London: Sage Publications.

Kemshall, H., Boeck, T. and Fleming, J. (2003) 'Young people, social capital and the negotiation of risk', seminar to the University of Sheffield Centre for Criminological Research (available at: www.shef.ac.uk/pathways-into-and-out-crime/reports/progress_report_project4.htm).

Kemshall, H., Mackenzie, G., Wood, J., Bailey, R. and Yates, J. (2005) *Strengthening the multi-agency public protection arrangements*, Practice and Development Report no 45, London: Home Office.

Kemshall, H. and Maguire, M. (2001) 'Public protection, partnership and risk penality: The multi-agency risk management of sexual and violent offenders', *Punishment and society*, vol 3, no 2, pp 237–64.

Kemshall, H., Marsland, L., Boeck, T. and Dunkerton, L. (2006) 'Young people, pathways and crime: Beyond risk factors', *Australian and New Zealand Journal of Criminology*, vol 39, no 3, pp 354–70.

Kemshall, H. and Wood, J. (forthcoming) 'Partnership for public protection: Key issues in the multi-agency public protection arrangements (MAPPA)', in C. Clark and J. McGhee (eds) *Private and confidential? Handling personal information in social and health services*, Bristol: The Policy Press.

Laub, J.H. and Sampson, R.J. (2001) 'Understanding desistance from crime', in M. Tonry (ed), *Crime and justice: A review of research, vol 28*, Chicago: University of Chicago Press.

Leavitt, G. (1999) 'Criminological theory as an art form: Implications for criminal justice policy', *Crime and Delinquency*, vol 45, no 3, pp 389–99.

Lipsey, M.W. and Wilson, D.B. (1993) 'The efficacy of psychological, educational, and behavioural treatment: Confirmation from meta-analysis', *American Psychologist*, vol 48, no 12, pp 1181–209.

Lipsey, M.W. and Wilson, D.B. (1999) 'Effective interventions with serious juvenile offenders', in R.E. Loeber and E.P. Farrington (eds), *Serious and violent juvenile offenders*, London: Sage Publications, pp 313–45.

Loeber, R. and Le Blanc, M. (1990) 'Toward a developmental criminology', in M. Tonry and N. Morris (eds), *Crime and Justice, vol 12*, Chicago: University of Chicago Press, 375-473.

Maruna, S. (2001) *Making good: How ex-convicts reform and rebuild their lives*, Washington DC: American Psychological Association.

May, C. (1999) *Explaining reconviction following a community sentence: The role of social factors*, Home Office Research Study 192, London: Home Office.

Morgan, R. (2006) 'Youth justice system "in crisis"' (available at: www.newsvote.bbc.co.uk, 24 October 2006, accessed 16 November 2006).

Muncie, J. (1999) 'Youth justice: Institutionalized intolerance: Youth justice and the 1998 Criminal Justice Act', *Critical Social Policy*, vol 19, no 2, pp 147–75.

Muncie, J. (2004) 'Youth justice: Responsibilities and rights', in J. Roche, S. Tucker, R. Thomson and R. Flynn (eds), *Youth in society*, London: Sage Publications.

Muncie, J. (2005) 'The globalisation of crime control: The case of youth and juvenile justice', *Theoretical Criminology*, vol 9, no 1, pp 35–64.

Muncie, J. (2006) 'Governing young people: Coherence and contradiction in contemporary youth justice', *Critical Social Policy*, vol 26, no 4, pp 770–93.

Murray, C. (1990) *The emerging British underclass*, London: IEA Health and Welfare Unit.

Nacro (2003) *A failure of youth justice: Reducing child imprisonment*, London: Nacro.

Nacro (2005) *A better alternative: Reducing child imprisonment*, London: Nacro.

O'Malley, P. (2004) 'The uncertain promise of risk', *Australian and New Zealand Journal of Criminology*, vol 37, no 3, pp 23–43.

O'Malley, P. (2006) 'Criminology and risk', in G. Mythen and S. Walklate (eds), *Beyond the risk society*, Maidenhead: Open University Press, pp 43-59.

Pitts, J. (2000) 'The new youth justice and the politics of electoral anxiety', in B. Goldson (ed), *The new youth justice*, Lyme Regis: Russell House Publishing.

Pitts, J. (2003) *The new politics of youth crime: Discipline or solidarity*, 2nd edn, London: Russell House Publishing.

Rhodes, T. (1997) 'Risk theory in epidemic times: Sex, drugs and the social organisation of "risk behaviour"', *Sociology of Health and Illness*, vol 19, no 2, pp 737–48.

Richards, D. and Smith, A. (2000) 'Violent young people detained in maximum security psychiatric hospital', in G. Boswell (ed), *Violent children and adolescents: Asking the questions why*, London: Whurr Publishers, pp 121–38.

Rutter, M. (1990) 'Psychosocial resilience and protective mechanisms', in J. Rolf, A.S. Masten, D. Chiccetti, K.H. Nuechterlein and S. Weintraub (eds), *Risk and protective factors in the development of psychopathology*, Cambridge: Cambridge University Press, pp 181-214.

Sampson, R.J. and Laub, J.H. (1993) *Crime in the making: Pathways and turning points through life*, Cambridge, MA: Harvard University Press.

Schoon, I. and Bynner, J. (2003) 'Risk and resilience in the life course: Implications for interventions and social policies', *Journal of Youth Studies*, vol 6, no 1, pp 21–31.

Scraton, P. and Haydon, D. (2002) 'Challenging the criminalization of children and young people: Securing a rights based agenda', in J. Muncie, G. Hughes and E. McLaughlin (eds), *Youth justice: Critical readings*, London: Sage Publications.

Sharland, E. (2006) 'Young people, risk taking and risk making', *British Journal of Social Work*, vol 36, no 2, pp 247–65.

Smith, R. (2003) *Youth justice: Ideas, policy and practice*, Cullompton: Willan.

Smith, R. (2006) 'Actuarialism and early intervention in contemporary youth justice', in B. Goldson and J. Muncie (eds), *Youth crime and justice: Critical issues*, London: Sage Publications.

Social Exclusion Unit (2000a) *National strategy for neighbourhood renewal: A framework for consultation*, London: Cabinet Office.

Social Exclusion Unit (2000b) *Report of policy action team 8: Anti-social behaviour*, London: Stationery Office.

Swadner, B.B. and Lubeck, S. (1995) 'The social construction of children and their families "at risk": An introduction', in B.B. Swadner and S. Lubeck (eds), *Children and families 'at promise': Deconstructing the discourse of risk*, New York: State University of New York Press, pp 1-21.

Tait, G. (1995) 'Shaping the "at risk youth": Risk, governmentality and the finn report', *Discourse*, vol 16, no 1, pp 123–34.

Thomas, T. (2005) *Sex crime: Sex offending and society*, Cullompton: Willan.

Tonry, M. (2004) *Punishment and politics: Evidence and emulation in the making of English crime control policy*, Cullompton: Willan.

Whyte, B. (2003) 'Young and persistent: Recent developments in youth justice policy and practice in Scotland', *Youth Justice*, vol 3, pp 74–85.

Wikström, P.-O. (2002) *Adolescent crime in context (The Peterborough youth study)*, report to the Home Office, Cambridge: Institute of Criminology, Cambridge.

Wikström, P.-O.H. (2004a) 'Crime as alternative: Towards a cross-level situational action theory of crime causation', in J. McCord (ed) *Beyond empiricism: Institutions and intentions in the study of crime*, New Brunswick: Transaction, pp 1-38.

Wikström, P.-O.H. (2004b) 'The origins of patterns in offending. Towards a developmental ecological action theory of crime involvement', in D.P. Farrington (ed), *Testing integrated developmental/life course theories of offending*, Advances in Criminological Theory, New Brunswick, NJ: Transaction.

Wood, J. and Kemshall, H. with Maguire, M., Hudson, K. and Mackenzie, G. (2007) *The operation and experience of multi-agency public protection arrangements*, London: Home Office, RDS.

Wright Mills, C. (1970) *The sociological imagination*, London: Penguin.

Yates, J. (2004) 'Criminological ethnography: Risks, dilemmas and their negotiation', *British Journal of Community Justice*, vol 3, no 1, pp 19–31.

Yates, J. (2006) 'An ethnography of youth and crime in a working class community', PhD thesis, Leicester: De Montfort University.

Youth Justice Board (2001) *Risk and protective factors associated with youth crime and effective interventions*, London: Youth Justice Board for England and Wales.

Youth Justice Board (2005) *Risk and protective factors*, London: Youth Justice Board.

Risk in practice: systems and practitioner judgement

2

Kerry Baker

Introduction

This chapter considers how practitioners in criminal justice agencies make complex decisions about risk within the current highly charged climate of political and media concern about public protection. The aim is not to look simply at questions of procedure, for example whether practitioners complete assessments within the required timescales, as these are investigated elsewhere (HMIP, 2006c and 2006d), but to develop a richer discussion of how practitioners make difficult judgements about risk. In this analysis, 'risk' refers predominantly to the risk of harm that a young person may present to others (the general public, named individuals or staff) although many of the issues would also be relevant to discussion of assessments of vulnerability or risk of self-harm and suicide.

The kind of scrutiny and public concern that has long been focused on decisions made by social workers about child protection is now being applied to criminal justice decisions about risk; but how much is known about how practitioners actually make such assessments? To what extent do current organisational goals and specified procedures for practice in criminal justice settings – in particular the use of structured assessment tools – shape the decision-making processes of practitioners? It is a key argument of this chapter that, while the core assessment tools used in youth justice and probation services (Asset and OASys) have helped to improve assessment quality, further consideration now needs to be given to ways of deepening knowledge and improving analysis rather than just collecting more information.

Assessment and prediction

The use of tools to predict offending behaviour is not a new development but although numerous studies have shown the superior predictive accuracy of actuarial methods compared to clinical approaches (Grove et al, 2000), there are several important caveats to note. Meehl argues that statistical methods outperform clinical approaches with regard to the prediction of 'somewhat heterogeneous, crude, socially defined behaviour outcomes' (1966: 122). The question of whether a young person is reconvicted within one or two years from the date of an assessment could be an example of this type of outcome. Meehl also points out, however, that a practitioner's creation of 'moment to moment clinical predictions' (1966: 126) may be more relevant than statistical calculations to the day-to-day management of cases. Another area in which the success of statistical methods has been limited – and which is of particular relevance to this chapter – is in relation to the prediction of particularly serious or dangerous behaviour (Monahan, 1996).

If it is difficult to provide accurate statistical predictions of the likelihood of very serious offences occurring, then it is necessary to have other ways of considering the risks that young people may present to others. It is also important to bear in mind the distinction between assessment and prediction with the former being a much broader process. To take the example of youth justice, the key tasks in assessment have been identified as follows:

- collecting information from a range of sources;
- recording information clearly and consistently;
- analysing information;
- presenting conclusions;
- sharing information;
- reviewing and updating assessments (Youth Justice Board, 2002).

A full assessment of the risk that a young person might pose to other people therefore requires a wide range of activities and involves more than simply a statistical calculation. This chapter focuses in particular on two of these tasks, namely how practitioners collect and analyse information.

Risk/need assessment tools, Asset and OASys

An account of the way in which assessment tools have come to have such a significant role in criminal justice agencies can and should take account of developments in both the tools themselves (Andrews et al, 2006) and in the organisational cultures that have encouraged their use (Nash, Chapter 6 in this volume). A key development in the design of assessment tools has been the transition from actuarial tools based largely on historic factors to risk/need tools that incorporate both static and dynamic components.

Much of the early impetus for the use of structured assessment tools in probation came from local services but it subsequently developed into a more centrally driven agenda with the development of the Offender Assessment System, OASys (Home Office, 2002). In the world of youth justice, one of the early initiatives of the Youth Justice Board (YJB) was to commission the design of a standard assessment profile (Asset[1]) for young people who offend aged 10–17 (Baker, 2005). Such tools were

---

[1] Unlike OASys, Asset is not an acronym.

seen as a means of enhancing defensible decision making and ensuring greater consistency in assessment practice. In terms of the design of these assessment tools 'risk of reconviction has played a more significant part in the development of risk/ need tools than risk of harm' (Merrington, 2004: 58). More recently, however, both OASys and Asset have been amended to include more on risk of harm to others (National Probation Service, 2006; Youth Justice Board, 2006).

The analysis that follows in this chapter focuses on assessments of young people (informed by relevant findings from research into both probation and social work practice) so it is therefore helpful to consider briefly the design of the tool used by youth justice practitioners. Asset is the standard assessment framework used by all Youth Offending Teams (YOTs) in England and Wales with young people who offend. It was introduced by the YJB in April 2000 alongside the launch of multidisciplinary YOTs to help promote comprehensive and consistent assessment practice with young people (Baker, 2004a). It aims to identify key risk factors contributing to a young person's offending behaviour but also the protective factors that might help to reduce the risk of reoffending. Practitioners are asked to give numerical ratings to indicate the extent to which they judge that particular risk factors are associated with the likelihood of further offending but, crucially, they are also expected to provide evidence to explain the basis for these ratings.

Asset does not attempt to provide a statistical prediction of risk of serious harm to others. The score that Asset produces relates to the likelihood of reconviction (Baker et al, 2003) but not to the level of harm likely to be caused by the offending behaviour. Rather than trying to provide a calculation of possible serious harm, the focus in this element of Asset is on providing a framework to help practitioners consider, for each individual case, key risk factors for behaviours that cause serious harm to others.

The core Asset profile (completed on all young people for whom a pre-sentence report or referral order report is prepared) contains a section on 'indicators of serious harm to others', which is a screening process to highlight cases where further assessment may be required (Youth Justice Board, 2006). If any of these indicators apply, a full 'Risk of Serious Harm' (ROSH) form should be completed. This begins with a series of questions about previous behaviour (not just offences but behaviour in a range of settings such as at home or school). It then moves on to a section about current risk indicators, for example concerning a young person's attitudes, circumstances and ongoing patterns of behaviour. This forms the basis for the conclusions in which the assessor tries to identify the types of serious offences that the young person might commit, who the victims might be, how significant the impact would be and the imminence of such behaviour occurring. In each section, assessors are asked to give evidence to justify their reasoning and judgements. Unlike tools used in related areas of practice (such as mental health; see Bailey et al, Chapter 4 in this volume) Asset does not try to produce a diagnosis of any particular condition but instead provides an assessment framework that is relevant to a wide range of young people and patterns of behaviour.

Evidence of assessment in practice

This chapter presents data from Asset ROSH forms completed by practitioners from a national sample of YOTs (Baker, 2004b). Quantitative data were collected from 300 completed ROSH forms but this chapter focuses primarily on the qualitative data gathered from a smaller sample. Forty cases (taken from 10 teams) were examined in more detail by analysing the narrative text in the evidence boxes of the ROSH forms and conducting semi-structured interviews with the relevant assessors. The aim of the analysis was essentially descriptive and, more particularly, was intended to answer the following questions:

- What factors did YOT staff consider when making such assessments and which did they consider the most important?
- What type of predictions were they making and how were these evidenced?
- How was Asset being used in this assessment process?

Most of the data were collected several years ago and it could be argued that assessment practice has improved since then, for example reflecting recent guidance and training on managing risk in the community (Youth Justice Board, 2005). However, evidence from inspection reports (HMIP, 2006c) and analysis of serious incidents (Blyth, Chapter 5 in this volume) reveals ongoing deficiencies in practice and therefore the findings from this study continue to be relevant.

Collecting information

Sources of information

Munro provides an interesting study of the reports from 45 public inquiries relating to (social work) errors in child abuse cases between 1973 and 1994. She demonstrates a reduction in 'investigation criticism' (1998: 91) in these reports over time as inter-agency communication and information gathering improved, partly through the introduction of checklists and more standardised procedures. However, she then goes on to argue that '[i]mprovements in collecting information have not been matched by improvements in assessments. To use the jigsaw analogy again, social workers have become better at drawing together the relevant pieces but have difficulty in fitting them together to form a picture of the family' (Munro, 1998: 91).

It would obviously be unrealistic to suggest that information collection in criminal justice is always adequate – examples of recent serious offences committed by offenders while under statutory supervision show some continuing problems here (HMIP, 2006a and 2006b) – but it is not unreasonable to suggest that the use of Asset and OASys increases the likelihood of relevant information being obtained. Indeed, both tools include a section on 'sources of information' in which assessors have to indicate where information has come from. This provides a prompt to remind practitioners of the various potential sources that could be used and also allows managers to identify if any particular items of information are routinely being missed.

Encouragingly, in this study of YOT practice there were some positive signs regarding the range of information sources used in assessments. Examples included staff from other agencies, family members, local media (for example, reports about the psychological damage experienced by the elderly victim of a burglary), and a home visit where the practitioner's observation conflicted with information provided by the young person and the assessor used the evidence box to explain the contradiction. However, no reference was made to the young person's self-assessment form ('What do YOU think?') in any of the ROSH forms or the staff interviews.

Sources of knowledge

In making judgements, practitioners may use arguments drawn from diverse sources such as theory, policy, values, a client's stated wish, empirical evidence or practical experience (Rosen et al, 1995). In this sample there was little evidence of theory being used explicitly but some suggestions of its role in influencing judgements implicitly, similar to the findings from a study of probation practice (Kemshall, 1998).

References to practical experience could be couched in general terms, for example, "Asset prompts some good questions, but as a social worker, these would be in the forefront of my mind anyway". Other staff referred in interview to more particular types of experience, which they felt shaped their assessments, for example, "… experience in probation and specialist work with sex offenders – I've also done child protection". Reliance on hunches or 'gut feelings' is a particularly interesting issue. For example, one assessor drew on his own and others' experience to state that, despite a current lack of clear evidence, he believed that experience of abuse might be a possibility in a particular case: "no evidence of abuse, however concerns from myself and other professionals regarding these offences, what brought it about, where did he learn this behaviour". This is similar to the pattern observed by Kemshall, who noted that probation officers 'placed a high degree of trust in their experience' (1998: 155) when undertaking risk assessments.

In a study of child protection assessments undertaken by social workers, Benbenishty et al (2003) found that empirical knowledge was rarely, if ever, cited by staff. A similar result was found in relation to Asset, with only one practitioner making explicit reference to this during an interview.

However, Sheppard and Ryan suggest that 'while direct reference to research was rare, it may be that such direct reference underestimates the true frequency of research use' (2003: 166). Practitioners may therefore be drawing on research knowledge without this being explicitly stated – it can often be difficult to discern what types of knowledge people are using: research and empirical evidence, personal experience or impressions picked up from colleagues.

Practitioners' different experiences and their individual knowledge of research findings will clearly affect the types of arguments and evidence they use. Completion of Asset is also influenced by contexts and cultures. The lack of reference to 'policy', for example (one of the categories identified by Rosen et al, 1995), was probably due to the fact that few YOTs had any established procedures for risk management at the time this study was undertaken. This might be different now that there is a clearer expectation from the YJB that YOTs should have policies on risk management (Youth Justice Board, 2005).

Analysing information

> In the early reports, it was assumed that if the information had been collated then the risk to the child would have been seen. This is not borne out by later inquiries where assessments are still heavily criticized, suggesting that social workers have an inadequate grasp of the theoretical knowledge needed to make sense of the information they gather. (Munro, 1998: 92)

Does Munro's argument that progress by social workers in collecting information has not been matched by improvements in analysis have validity in youth justice? Asset requires assessors to provide evidence to support judgements and ratings but the temptation to miss out or skirt over the evidence boxes in Asset was one that practitioners readily acknowledged in interview: 'But then again, 'any odd or disconcerting behaviour', it's easy to tick that and not explain what it is' (Baker, 2004b: 244). An in-depth look at the extent and quality of evidence and analysis recorded by practitioners is now required.

Combining disparate items of information

Sheppard et al (2001: 865) make a distinction between 'partial case hypotheses', which relate to particular aspects of a case or situation, and 'whole case hypotheses', which attempt to bring together different issues into a coherent explanation for the case as a whole. They suggest that such hypotheses are an essential feature of a full assessment.

There were some examples of YOT staff attempting to do this, but in many cases there was little evidence to indicate that assessors were trying to draw together different pieces of information. In one case, for example, the ROSH form listed a range of quite disturbing behaviours. The young person committed a burglary against a neighbour's house and then started a fire inside the bedroom. He had been known to hit teachers, to carry a knife and to be violent towards peers. There was also a range of incidents involving cruelty to animals: "he has stabbed a cat, a guinea pig, nearly strangled a child and has actually strangled a rabbit. Put a steel pole through a gerbil's ears and put a cat in the freezer because it scratched him."

While it is positive that the assessor identified these different types of problematic behaviour as being relevant, there was little attempt to link them together. For example, separate references were made to his violent behaviour towards peers and to instances of cruelty to animals, but there was no attempt to consider whether there might be a common explanation for these two problematic behaviours.[2]

A second example is taken from the 'analysis of offending section' of a completed Asset form:

> **During school mid morning break one of John's friends approached an older pupil to ask him for a light for a cigarette. He responded in a verbally aggressive manner and when John and his friend challenged him he threw a punch at them. John then threatened him with a knife and accidentally stabbed him.**

This young person was aged 12 at the time of the offence but there was no discussion in Asset about why he was carrying a knife. In the 'family and personal relationships' section of the form there was a reference to the fact that the young person's elder brother had recently completed a two-year custodial sentence for armed robbery, but there was no analysis of any possible link between this and John's use of a weapon. These examples of 'information treated discretely' (Reder et al, 1993: 84) illustrate how assessors can have different pieces of information available but not combine them effectively within Asset to provide a more complete picture of a case.

Considering different possibilities

Writing in the context of social work practice, Sheppard (1995) argues that the process of making assessments should involve generating hypotheses to understand

---

[2] There is increasing evidence of a link between animal cruelty and other violent behaviour (Office of Juvenile Justice and Delinquency Prevention, 2001)

and explain the information available in any particular case. There is conflicting evidence from empirical studies on the extent to which practitioners actually use such an approach. Sheppard et al found that while some social workers generated a number of hypotheses about individual cases and compared these in order to find the best 'fit' with the available evidence, others remained fixed with 'one particular idea about how the situation was to be understood, or no particular idea at all' (2001: 871). In the context of probation practice, Kemshall found that the process of generating and falsifying hypotheses was the exception rather than the rule and instead 'the mode of inquiry appears to reflect … the closed professional system in which information is matched to existing beliefs' (1998: 159).

This highlights the problems associated with assessors seeking evidence to confirm initial suppositions rather than giving full consideration to a range of possible explanations. In situations such as child protection or assessments of risk of serious harm to others in which the potential outcomes are so serious, Sheppard et al are surely right to argue that 'this commitment to one particular hypothesis … may give cause for concern' (2001: 871). However, perhaps it is time to consider whether assessment tools such as Asset and OASys give the impression that there is one correct answer or one 'defensible decision' that practitioners have to find. Do staff feel that they need to have everything worked out before they can complete the assessment profile? This is certainly the impression given by one youth justice worker who, in describing a particular case involving some (apparently) serious behaviour, commented, "Because I haven't been able to figure it out I haven't filled in that bit".

Both Asset and OASys require assessors to describe the likelihood of a young person causing serious harm to others and to specify, as far as possible, the circumstances in which this is most likely to occur. Examples from ROSH forms illustrate the kinds of description that practitioners used when making such predictions about potential future behaviour (such as 'when seeking to self-affirm, gain status or to demonstrate personal efficacy' or 'if money/material items are refused her and she feels rejected').

However, although both tools include questions about what factors might increase or decrease risk *and* the guidance emphasises the importance of regularly reviewing assessments, it may be that not enough attention has been paid to 'how resistant people are to altering their beliefs' (Munro, 1996: 799). This is a logical extension of the discussion above concerning multiple hypotheses for, as Sheppard suggests, if such an approach were used, assessors would be alert to 'disconfirming data' and ready to reformulate hypotheses in the light of new evidence (1995: 275). Why is this so rarely seen in practice? Perhaps it is partly because of the perception of a blame culture and the consequent development of defensive practice (Tuddenham, 2000) in which speculation about a variety of possible options might be seen as a lack of competence in reaching decisions about risk levels.

A second reason might be to do with the considerable difficulty of thinking and working in this way:

> The social worker does not just face altering his or her belief about one item of information but has to consider changing the whole picture of the case. All the known evidence then needs to be reappraised and found a place in the new emerging picture. The human tendency to avoid critical reappraisals of their beliefs may in part be due to reluctance to undertake such *a challenging and arduous intellectual task*. (Munro, 1996: 800, emphasis added)

Thirdly, the implications of adopting this mode of thinking need to be considered in the light of everyday operational policies and procedures. Sheppard et al refer to practitioners imagining 'the possibilities and the consequences of these possibilities' and formulating 'client behaviour hypotheses' (2000: 478). These are essentially speculations 'about the client's behaviour, including how they will behave in particular situations' (Sheppard et al, 2000: 479). However, encouraging speculative development of hypotheses may clash with practitioners' concerns to avoid labelling young people or disseminating information that may be detrimental to them.

It is important to acknowledge that some of these concerns are genuine and not necessarily just a reflection of poor practice. The rather mundane but inescapably relevant issue of caseloads and working conditions cannot be ignored either:

> If this impression of maingrade staff working at the limits of their abilities is correct (and from personal experience we have no reason to doubt it), then the potential consequences could be serious – if OASys is completed badly, risk assessment will be compromised, inappropriate allocation to programmes will occur, and the public will be at greater risk. (Mair et al, 2006: 21)

A clear example of this was seen in the case of Damien Hanson,[3] where mistakes were clearly made by probation staff but these occurred at a time when the service was experiencing numerous staff shortages that resulted in a senior probation officer trying to manage two teams at once (HMIP, 2006a). There may be times when the practical pressure of having to 'get the job done' takes precedence over the ideal of staff critically analysing multiple hypotheses.

Conclusion

Practitioners' level of compliance with procedures is important but is not enough on its own to produce in-depth assessments of young people who may present a serious risk to others. Similarly, reports into practice (or failings in practice) that

---

[3] Hanson was convicted of committing murder after being released on parole licence.

focus only on observance of required procedures cannot provide a thorough understanding of how decisions are being made. One example of this would be the report into the supervision of Peter Williams[4] by Nottingham City YOT (HMIP, 2005) which, as Nellis (2006) rightly points out, concentrates almost entirely on procedural compliance without giving much attention to the question of whether staff had the appropriate levels of understanding, knowledge and ability to work with challenging and often highly troubled young people.

It is sometimes questioned (Nash, Chapter 6 in this volume) whether the focus on public protection in criminal justice, and the relatively small number of young people who present a risk of serious harm to others, has adversely affected the way in which *all* young people who offend are treated. A full discussion is outside the scope of this chapter but there is a strong argument for saying that the emphasis on in-depth assessment of high-risk cases could in fact have benefits for other young people if it leads to a general improvement in analysis and decision-making skills. This chapter has attempted to explore in some detail the knowledge and thinking processes used by practitioners when making complex judgements about risk. Further studies would be valuable in adding to our understanding of, for example, YOT practitioners' judgements of suicide risk or how OASys has affected the way in which probation staff make judgements of risk posed by adults who offend.

Whatever the precise model of practice or assessment tool used, there will always be some element of uncertainty in decision making. As in related areas of practice (like child protection) the process of assessment will be impaired by factors such as incompleteness of information, time constraints, contradictory or misleading data, and may also be hindered by a lack of 'clear empirical findings', 'unequivocal professional knowledge' and 'explicit guidelines' (Benbenishty et al, 2003: 138).

While the provision of guidelines and policies for staff to follow has perhaps improved, it is time to look more fundamentally at the types of knowledge that practitioners use and the thinking skills required. One obvious area to consider is the design of the assessment tools themselves and the training that underpins their use. The evidence suggests that there are some critical questions that practitioners may not routinely be considering when trying to analyse information collected in a particular case, such as:

- questions about the reliability of evidence;
- questions about the links between disparate pieces of information;
- whether there are alternative hypotheses that need to be considered.

It would be possible to add reflective questions to Asset and OASys on such issues. For example: are there any other possible explanations for this behaviour?

---

[4] Williams was convicted of a murder, committed while he was under statutory supervision by the YOT.

What would it take to falsify your prediction? What other outcomes are possible and what is the likelihood of them occurring? The procedures for reviewing and updating assessments could also be amended, for example, to incorporate more of an expectation that decisions and judgements will have changed over time so that it becomes easier for assessors to 'admit' that their initial conclusions may have been mistaken or incomplete.

However, to what extent is it the role of assessment tools to promote such reflective, critical practice? How much reliance should be placed on the tools and how much on other aspects of professional development (such as training)? How does an assessor's knowledge of theory and research affect the way they complete an Asset or OASys? Much depends on how assessment tools are applied, for example, how much discretion do staff have in using a tool and interpreting the results (Baker, 2005)?

The role of managers in providing feedback for staff on the quality of assessments is also critical. Lack of discussion about particular cases can be a problem, as highlighted by a practitioner who commented that:

> **We never have the chance really to sit down and review what's going on. There's quality control by managers but mine have come back with no issues raised in terms of how I'm filling it in on ROSH so I don't know how much managers know. I just keep doing what I do.**

Another problem may be that the only type of feedback received by practitioners is essentially negative: 'The information generated by this activity rarely returns to workers in any shape or form, or if it does, it is to highlight areas for improvement in delivery or practice as opposed to what is working – it is negative information' (Watson, 2002: 883). This is especially pertinent in the current climate, in which serious incidents can attract extensive political and media attention and prompt a search for someone to blame.

'Facts on their own are silent. Social workers need to know relevant theories and research to interpret the facts and formulate assessments of risk or family functioning' (Munro, 1998: 92). If this is so, how could empirical evidence and research findings be disseminated to youth justice and probation staff more effectively? Do current training programmes place enough emphasis on theoretical concepts or does the current trend for modular, competency-based training mean that practitioners are not given the opportunity to develop a coherent, comprehensive overview of relevant research and theory?

While there is much talk about the fact that risk should be seen as 'dynamic', perhaps the current tools and systems do not adequately reflect this and there remains a danger of practitioners seeking unrealistic 'right answers' in this complex and fraught arena. To what extent should practitioners be permitted, or even encouraged, to remain uncertain?

> Social workers like other professionals strive for conditions of certainty. And, at times, they must act as though certainty is easy to come by, for example, when children or adults are perceived to be in great danger. However, we want to press the point that in a great many situations, the 'certain' thing is not necessarily the right thing. To counteract this tendency to make judgements too soon and to look only for evidence that supports the decision, *practitioners need to stay in uncertainty for longer*, and to assess whether, because of the circumstances, there is a need to hold on to doubt whilst taking the time to seek out other possible versions. (Taylor and White, 2006: 944, emphasis added)

Although this may be an intuitively appealing position to adopt, there is clearly a difficult dilemma between the need to make decisions in order to take practical action while also remaining open to new information and the possibility of falsified hypotheses. While it may be generally agreed that the 'aim of assessment is to guide action' (Reder et al, 1993: 83) 'the pressure to 'handle cases quickly and efficiently' may predispose social workers to use formal knowledge in a way that shores up their 'anchor hypothesis' when we may want to encourage them to use theory or research findings to shake up or destabilize precipitously formed judgments' (Taylor and White, 2006: 946). Similarly, Asset and OASys need to balance competing demands; they need to be tools that promote critical thinking, but if they are to be clearly linked to practical action they still need to lead towards a conclusion rather than just a list of possible alternative outcomes.

The evidence suggests that improvements are needed in the quality of assessments made by practitioners. However, any policy initiatives need to take into account the complex circumstances in which such decisions are often made and the difficult tension between the need to intervene and the importance of seeing assessment as an ongoing process. Further refinement of assessment tools such as Asset and OASys can help in this process but attention also needs to be given to the organisational and professional cultures that shape the way in which practitioners think about, reflect upon and analyse information.

References

Andrews, D., Bonta, J. and Wormith, J.S. (2006) 'The recent past and near future of risk and/or need assessment', *Crime & Delinquency*, vol 52, no 1, pp 7–27.

Baker, K. (2004a) 'Is *Asset* really an asset? Assessment of young offenders in practice', in R. Burnett and C. Roberts (eds), *What works in probation and youth justice: Developing evidence based practice*, Cullompton: Willan, pp 70–87.

Baker, K. (2004b) 'Risk assessment of young offenders', unpublished PhD thesis, Oxford: University of Oxford.

Baker, K. (2005) 'Assessment in youth justice: Professional discretion and the use of Asset', *Youth Justice*, vol 5, no 2, pp 106–22.

Baker, K., Jones, S., Roberts, C. and Merrington, S. (2003) *Validity and reliability of Asset*, London: Youth Justice Board.

Benbenishty, R., Osmo, R. and Gold, N. (2003) 'Rationale provided for risk assessments and for recommended interventions in child protection: A comparison between Canadian and Israeli professionals', *British Journal of Social Work*, vol 33, no 2, pp 137–55.

Grove, W., Zald, D., Lebow, B., Snitz, B. and Nelson, C. (2000) 'Clinical vs mechanical prediction: A meta-analysis', *Psychological Assessment*, vol 12, no 1, pp 19–30.

HMI Probation (2005) *Inquiry into the supervision of Peter Williams by Nottingham City Youth Offending Team*, London: HMI Probation.

HMI Probation (2006a) *An independent review of a serious further offence case: Damien Hanson & Elliot White*, London: HMI Probation.

HMI Probation (2006b) *Anthony Rice: An independent review of a serious further offence case*, London: HMI Probation.

HMI Probation (2006c) *Joint inspection of Youth Offending Teams: Annual report 2005–2006*, London: HMI Probation.

HMI Probation (2006d) *Joint thematic inspection report: Putting risk of harm in context*, London: HMI Probation.

Home Office (2002) *Introduction to OASys*, National Probation Service Briefing 2, London: National Probation Service.

Kemshall, H. (1998) *Risk in probation practice*, Aldershot: Ashgate.

Mair, G., Burke, L. and Taylor, S. (2006) 'The worst tax form you've ever seen? Probation officers' views about OASys', *Probation Journal*, vol 53, no 1, pp 7–23.

Meehl, P. (1966) *Clinical versus statistical prediction: A theoretical analysis and a review of the evidence*, Minneapolis: University of Minnesota Press.

Merrington, S. (2004) 'Assessment tools in probation: Their development and potential', in R. Burnett and C. Roberts (eds), *What works in probation and youth justice: Developing evidence based practice*, Cullompton: Willan, pp 46–69.

Monahan, J. (1996) 'Violence prediction: The past twenty and the next twenty years', *Criminal Justice and Behavior*, vol 23, no 1, pp 107–20.

Munro, E. (1996) 'Avoidable and unavoidable mistakes in child protection work', *British Journal of Social Work*, vol 26, no 6, pp 793–808.

Munro, E. (1998) 'Improving social workers' knowledge base in child protection work', *British Journal of Social Work*, vol 28, no 1, pp 89–105.

National Probation Service (2006) *OASys manual: Revised chapter on risk of serious harm (Chapter 8)*, London: National Probation Service.

Nellis, M. (2006) 'The limitations of electronic monitoring: Reflections on the tagging of Peter Williams', *Prison Service Journal*, vol 164, pp 3–12.

Office of Juvenile Justice and Delinquency Prevention (2001) *Animal abuse and youth violence*, Washington, DC: US Department of Justice.

Reder, P., Duncan, S. and Gray, M. (1993) *Beyond blame: Child abuse tragedies revisited*, London: Routledge.

Rosen, A., Procter, E., Morrow-Howell, N. and Staudt, M. (1995) 'Rationales for practice decisions: Variations in knowledge use by decision task and social work service', *Research on Social Work Practice*, vol 5, no 4, pp 501–23.

Sheppard, M. (1995) 'Social work, social science and practice wisdom', *British Journal of Social Work*, vol 25, no 3, pp 265–93.

Sheppard, M., Newstead, S., Di Caccavo, A. and Ryan, K. (2000) 'Reflexivity and the development of process knowledge in social work: A classification and empirical study', *British Journal of Social Work*, vol 30, no 4, pp 465–88.

Sheppard, M., Newstead, S., Di Caccavo, A. and Ryan, K. (2001) 'Comparative hypothesis assessment and quasi triangulation as process knowledge assessment strategies in social work practice', *British Journal of Social Work*, vol 31, no 6, pp 863–85.

Sheppard, M. and Ryan, K. (2003) 'Practitioners as rule using analysts: A further development of process knowledge in social work', *British Journal of Social Work*, vol 33, vol 2, pp 157–76.

Taylor, C. and White, S. (2006) 'Knowledge and reasoning in social work: Educating for humane judgment', *British Journal of Social Work*, vol 36, no 6, pp 937–54.

Tuddenham, R. (2000) 'Beyond defensible decision-making: Towards reflexive assessment of risk and dangerousness', *Probation Journal*, vol 47, no 3, pp 173–83.

Watson, D. (2002) 'A critical perspective on quality within the personal social services: Prospects and concerns', *British Journal of Social Work*, vol 32, no 7, pp 877–91.

Youth Justice Board (2002) *Assessment, planning interventions and supervision: Key elements of effective practice (source document)*, London: Youth Justice Board.

Youth Justice Board (2005) *Managing risk in the community*, London: Youth Justice Board.

Youth Justice Board (2006) *Asset guidance*, London: Youth Justice Board.

Young people and violence: balancing public protection with meeting needs

3

Gwyneth Boswell

Introduction

In recent years there has been much political talk of the need to 'rebalance' the criminal justice system in favour of victims of crime. This ethos was given expression in the White Paper *Justice for all* (Home Office et al, 2002) and in the subsequent 2003 Criminal Justice Act that introduced new, lengthy custodial sentences for the express purpose of public protection. The need for public protection is determined by an assessment of dangerousness by the Crown Court at the point of sentence. 'Dangerousness' is defined as 'significant risk of serious harm to the public'; 'serious harm' is defined as '… death or serious personal injury, whether physical or psychological' (s224[3]). These new sentences, Detention for Public Protection (an indeterminate sentence) and the Extended Sentence for Public Protection, may be passed on both adults and young people who offend. This extends the range of long custodial sentences for juveniles, which were hitherto restricted to the detention that may be passed on them for murder and other 'grave crimes' under Section 90 and 91 (respectively) of the 2000 Powers of the Criminal Courts (Sentencing) Act.

While the desirability of the protection of potential victims from serious harm is not a matter for debate, what is perhaps more questionable is the contextual assumption that being harsher on perpetrators will necessarily always equate to greater benefits for victims and the wider community. A number of authors have expressed suspicion of this stance. For example, '[t]he attempt to justify harsher sentencing of offenders and curtailment of civil liberties in the name of victims is not new, and it is part of an international trend, but it has yet to be effectively challenged in England and Wales' (Williams and Canton, 2005: 2).

Further, Hedderman and Hough (2004) pose the question of whether it is 'getting tough or being effective' that matters. That is the issue, which this chapter seeks specifically to address in relation to young people and violence. In so doing, it will first examine the characteristics of young victims; secondly, the characteristics of young people who offend violently; thirdly, the links between the two; and finally the implications for balancing the protection of victims and potential victims with the appropriate means of reducing the 'dangerousness' of young perpetrators.

Young victims of violence

This section focuses upon young people under the age of 18 years, whom the law in England and Wales classifies as children. As a category they have tended to be somewhat overlooked in victimisation literature, with the spotlight focused rather on the types of crime that have been perpetrated upon them. However, as the Gulbenkian Report on Children and Violence noted, '... children suffer far more violent victimisation than do adults' (Calouste Gulbenkian Foundation, 1995: 256). The report argues that this level of victimisation is because of their largely dependent status, which renders them more vulnerable to 'conventional' crimes such as homicide and assault, to family violence including violent punishments, sexual abuse by parents and others, and assaults by siblings, and to institutional violence such as bullying in schools. To this list might be added well-catalogued instances of abuse and bullying in children's homes, secure units and juvenile young offender institutions (YOIs), in all of which children and adolescents have variously sustained racist attacks, other serious assaults including rape, and have in some cases died or committed suicide as a result (Goldson, 2002 and 2006). Some of these types of victimisation will now be considered.

Homicide

Homicide is the rarest but clearly the most serious crime to be committed on children. Reporting in 2003, Creighton and Tissier noted that criminal statistics for the previous 28 years showed an average of 79 child deaths per annum (babies being the most at risk); in 78% of these cases, parents are the principal suspects. Those killed by friends, acquaintances, other associates and strangers are very much in the minority.

However, criminal statistics probably constitute an underestimate of the prevalence of this particular crime in terms of the reporting, recording and analysis that lead to the final figure. For example, in the case of suspicious deaths of babies and younger children where parents deny guilt and there is insufficient evidence for a prosecution, open verdicts are usually recorded. Further to this, the annual mortality statistics published by the Office for National Statistics do not include rates for 16 and 17 year olds, who are at much higher risk of death than younger children.

Child abuse

In the UK, child abuse is generally recognised as belonging to one or more of the categories of physical, emotional, sexual abuse or neglect. As with child deaths, the prevalence of child abuse is generally believed to be seriously under-reported and recorded and also frequently to go unrecognised (Vizard, 2006). Recent figures suggest the following in relation to the year 1 April 2002 to 31 March 2003:

- There were 4,109 reported offences of 'cruelty or neglect of children' and 1,880 of 'gross indecency with a child under the age of 14' in England and Wales.
- There were 30,200 children's names added to child protection registers in England.
- There were 570,000 referrals concerning child maltreatment to social services departments in England.

A breakdown of all these cases shows the following proportions: neglect, 39%; physical abuse, 19%; emotional abuse, 18%; sexual abuse, 10%; mixed categories, 15% (Creighton, 2004). As in the case of child deaths, much of the abuse is parental.

Smacking

Within Europe, eight countries have now imposed a complete ban on the physical punishment of children. In England and Wales smacking remains legal but, since the 1998 Human Rights Act (incorporating the 1989 United Nations Convention on the Rights of the Child) came into force in October 2001, courts have been obliged to consider whether punishment amounts to 'reasonable chastisement'. The factors to be weighed are the nature and context of the treatment and its duration; its physical and mental effects and, in some circumstances, the sex, age and state of health of the victim.

At the same time, protection from harm is as much of a human rights issue for children as it is for adults – arguably more so as children are both smaller and more fragile. The Convention on the Rights of the Child may now have acquired the status of international law, but children cannot on their own seek justice through the courts when they are victimised (frequently behind the closed doors of their own family) and their Convention rights are breached. Nevertheless, in November 2004, a majority of MPs voted against an outright ban on smacking within the new Children Bill, and in favour of an amendment allowing light chastisement, with the caveat that no grazes, scratches, minor swellings, cuts or bruises should ensue. In the event that they do, the maximum sentence is five years' imprisonment. It was notable, however, that around the same time, the government allowed a free ('conscience') vote on foxhunting but retained its three-line whip on the question of physical punishment to children.

Victimisation on the basis of identity

As is the case for adults, some children are more likely to fall prey to victimisation by reason of identity-based characteristics such as gender, race, religion, disability and so on:

> Certain groups of children are particularly at risk of violence, including disabled children and children from some minority ethnic groups. Victimisation statistics in crime surveys and other interview research provide prima facie evidence of discrimination. Racial harassment, always a form of violence and often involving physical violence, threatens many children in the community and in schools (Calouste Gulbenkian Foundation, 1995: 115)

Children may be singled out for school bullying and find themselves victimised as members of families of black and ethnic minority origin and/or of minority religions. Added to this is the risk of such victimisation going unrecognised by schools and criminal justice agencies because of institutional racism, despite the requirement of the 2000 Race Relations (Amendment) Act for public bodies to have due regard to the need to eliminate unlawful racial discrimination. More recently, the misperception of Muslims as terrorists, linking them with Al-Qaeda and the attacks on the World Trade Center on 11 September 2001, has triggered well-documented victimisation and 'hate crime' towards Muslim families and communities. The Nottinghamshire Common Monitoring Scheme found that 11.4% of the victims of racially motivated crime were under the age of 10 years (MPTC, 1998). Other studies have shown the pervasion of racial bullying, harassment and attack across the lifespan, beginning in childhood (Bowling, 1998; Clancy et al, 2001; Garland and Chakraborti, 2004).

In terms of gender characteristics, a review of the research shows that boys are more vulnerable than girls to physical abuse and non-family assaults, while girls are more vulnerable than boys to sexual abuse (Calouste Gulbenkian Foundation, 1995). Female children are particularly (though of course not exclusively) likely to become the subjects of child pornography, and increasingly so on the internet, where it is fast becoming a major social problem. The debate surrounding the issue of what actually constitutes child pornography, and at what point viewing it actually becomes a crime, serves only to reduce the significance of the child victim concerned. Taylor and Quayle (2003) observe that the process of trying to understand an unpalatable phenomenon brings with it the accompanying danger of appearing to condone it. They also note the pervading tension between official reluctance to censor on the internet and obvious child protection issues, both set against the increasing sexualisation of girls in the media (Taylor and Quayle, 2003).

Research on children with disabilities has been sparse, but recent work has shown that they are a distinct high-risk group for victimisation and maltreatment, being on average two to three times more likely to be abused than non-disabled children (Little, 2004). Further, while they often come to the attention of the health services, their condition may mask the fact that they have been abused or otherwise victimised, thus undermining the quality of the assessment and treatment they receive.

Societal images of violence

Beyond any formal, legalised responses that society makes to its child victims are other powerful responses to be found, for example, in the media, which offer very mixed messages about crime, particularly violent crime. In the UK, this has had an impact upon the populace as a consequence of public inquiry either because of: abusive practices in children's homes, as discussed earlier, the mismanagement of suspected child abuse; or child death within or outside the family. High-profile examples in respect of the latter three arenas have included: Cleveland, where large numbers of children suspected of having been abused were taken into care, and the social work and health professionals vilified for unwarranted interference (Butler-Sloss, 1988); the long-term abuse and eventual murders in their families of Jasmine Beckford (Blom-Cooper, 1985) and Victoria Climbié (Laming, 2003), where professionals were accused of neglecting their duty of intervention; and the murders in Soham of Holly Wells and Jessica Chapman, where the failure of professionals to communicate and liaise effectively about a known sex offender was highlighted (Bichard, 2004).

According to the particular circumstances, then, those with professional responsibility have been criticised either for intervening too much or intervening too little. Public feeling seemingly runs as high about the increase of state interference in domestic and family life as it does about that same state's failure to prevent the death or abuse of a child. Cleveland or Climbié – which is worse? Either way, the child is the victim.

Power relations within and beyond UK societies have similarly institutionalised the victimisation of children. For example, governmental regimes predicated upon political oppressions have both portrayed violence as a behavioural norm for children and engaged them in it. In other parts of the world, child soldiers are the epitome of state-sanctioned violence for the young. The apartheid regime in South Africa prompted strikes and demonstrations by school children against 'Bantu Education' in 1976; the response of the authorities was to shoot them. In the Western world, children in Northern Ireland lived through the longest period of sustained conflict in recent times. In all these situations, children died, witnessed death, were maimed, lost parents through imprisonment, were themselves imprisoned and saw or used guns in their daily lives.

Further, violence is enshrined in the response of a range of justice systems to criminalised antisocial behaviour – that is to say torture and other forms of physical retribution, and capital punishment – all of which, in some countries, may be applied to children and young people, despite wide ratification of the 1989 UN Convention on the Rights of the Child. Similarly, reports from the Bureau of International Labor Affairs (1996, 1998, 2006) have shown that mental and physical violence to victims of child prostitution and child labour is to be seen not only in Asia, the Far East, Central and South America, as popularly imagined, but also in parts of the 'developed' Western world. Physical violence between family members is frequently seen as normal for many societies (Gelles and Straus, 1988). Most recently, the UN Secretary-General has brought a great deal of this kind of information together to demonstrate a worldwide failure to protect children either through legislation or state response, and regards this failure as a major threat to global development (UN Secretary-General, 2006).

At national and international levels, then, these issues raise fundamental questions about how societies treat and respond to young victims of violence, and how children more generally experience power and its applications. As John (2003) notes, democracies are created both in the public sphere and within the emotional intimacies of the family. In these settings, without either fully developed cognitive skills or legal standing, it is arguably highly problematic for children to engage in the process of recognising and realising their rightful autonomy and agency. So while the risk of becoming a victim of recorded crime in England and Wales may be falling (Garside, 2006), there is little sign of the new 'rebalancing' process doing very much to protect children and young people from violence within this particular society.

Young perpetrators of violence

> Shepherd: I would there were no age between sixteen and three-and-twenty, or that youth would sleep out the rest; for there is nothing in the between but getting wenches with child, wronging the ancientry, stealing, fighting. (Shakespeare, *The Winter's Tale*, III.iii.1533-57)

The foregoing quotation serves as an excellent reminder that adolescence is a developmental stage that may continue through and beyond the teenage years, during which it is not abnormal for antisocial behaviour to manifest itself, and in which the arrival at capacity for mature judgement seems likely to vary considerably from one young person to another. Even at the extreme end of adolescents who kill, Bailey points out:

> Whether focusing on normality or pathology within serious young offenders, there is the inevitable ebb and flow of adolescent behaviour and thought which are so difficult to define. Adolescence needs to be seen both as a context and as a phenomenon laying the foundation for an understanding of the unique developmental issues for the individual adolescent. (Bailey, 1996: 19)

Adolescence, then, serves as the broad backcloth to offending of any kind by young people. It is the lens through which they receive and respond to societal images of violence, described in the previous section. It reminds us that not only can young people's behaviour change for the worse, it is also susceptible to change for the better, and is thus worth a concerted investment for the future. In respect of the perpetration of violence, therefore, a significant part of that investment arguably lies in trying to discover the reasons for their offending, so that work can be done to eradicate these in the future.

It is important to note that violent (including sexual) offending exists on a continuum from common assault to murder and that those who commit it do not constitute a homogeneous group. The main predictor is being male. Although the evidence has taken time to accumulate, the risk factors for youth violence are by now well known, and are helpfully described in a recent review of the research by Lösel and Bender (2006). They note that many violent young people show persistent problem behaviour from an early age and they list the factors that can be instrumental in producing chain reactions if no protective factor, such as trusted adult support or educational achievement, intervenes. These include biological vulnerabilities; neuropsychological deficits; economic disadvantage; multiple stressors; family disharmony such as abuse, neglect, poor parenting and parental criminality; school failure; truancy; deviant peer groups and attitudes; aggression-prone social information processing; antisocial lifestyle; and deprived and violent neighbourhoods. As these factors accumulate and, at times, feed into each other, the stronger becomes the likelihood that serious problems such as violent manifestation will ensue. Young people with these kinds of profiles are very familiar to researchers and criminal justice professionals. They frequently embody the child victim, described in previous sections, and the adolescent perpetrator all in one person.

Victims who become perpetrators

Studies of violent young people in a range of countries have shown how the oppressed may evolve into the oppressor and the victim and the offender become located in one single, damaged young person (for example, Boswell, 1995 and 1996, in England and Wales; Widom and White, 1997, in the United States; Wedge et al, 2000 and Zwane, 2000, in South Africa). Although there are clearly differences that relate to cultural and political variables, these studies show remarkably similar retrospective patterns.

In England and Wales, during the 1990s, the author undertook a survey of the prevalence of abuse and loss in the lives of one third of the population of young people detained under Sections 53 (1) and (2) of the 1933 Children and Young Persons Act (Boswell, 1995 and 1996). The former group was detained for murder, the latter for other grave crimes; all were sentenced between the ages of 10-17 inclusive. The method adopted was to examine a random sample of 200 centrally held files, to note down professionally confirmed evidence in them of child abuse and loss and, where this evidence was partial or ambiguous, to interview the young people themselves about these issues. A total of 72% of respondents were found to have experienced abuse, divided as follows: emotional (28.5%); sexual (29%); physical (40%); organised/ritual (1.5%); combinations of abuses (27%).

A total of 57% had experienced significant loss via bereavement (21%) or cessation of contact, usually with a parent (43%) and, in a small number of cases, both. In only 18 out of 200 cases studied were there no personally reported evidences of abuse and/or loss. In other words, the total number of Section 53 young people who had experienced one or both phenomena was 91%. The total number who had experienced *both* abuse *and* loss was 35%, suggesting that the presence of a double childhood trauma may be a potent factor in the lives of young people who offend violently. Indeed, there seems little doubt that child abuse and childhood experience of loss, when no effective opportunity is provided for the child to make sense of these experiences, constitutes unresolved trauma that is likely to manifest itself in some way at a later date. Many children become depressed, disturbed, violent or all three, girls tending to internalise and boys to externalise their responses (American Psychiatric Association, 2000).

These findings were similar to those produced by Falshaw and Browne (1997) in a study of 70 boys and girls in a specialist secure unit. They found that 72% overall had a history of child maltreatment: of these, 34% had experienced sexual abuse; 58% physical abuse; 32% neglect; and 28% emotional abuse. Multiple and repeated victimisation was also found in over half the sample (Hamilton et al, 2002). In a recent review of the research evidence in the US and UK, Falshaw (2005) makes a persuasive case for the link between child maltreatment and subsequent offending and points out that the US has begun to address this link through counselling and other kinds of support to victims who have subsequently come into contact with the criminal justice system.

Case study

Not untypical of this group of young people is Michael, now aged 32, who was sentenced to a Section 53 (now Section 91) discretionary life sentence 15 years ago for offences of grievous bodily harm and attempted rape. His background contains almost every kind of abuse, but the experience that is most significant to him is the loss of his father, who had left home when Michael was three years old for reasons which Michael did not understand; they did not renew contact until relatively recently, during Michael's prison sentence. The day Michael's father left, his mother beat Michael, and such beatings continued several times a week, until he was taken into care at the age of 10 years. He has very little memory of his life between the ages of five and seven years. His elder sister, however, tells him that he and she were both severely sexually abused by one of their mother's lovers during that period, and also that, on one occasion, Michael was nearly strangled. Michael himself has no memory of that incident, but does know that he has panic attacks and on some occasions blackouts if anyone touches his neck. He also has nightmares about being strangled. One of his worst memories is of his mother locking him in the cellar for two hours. The cellar contained rats and he recounts an experience of sheer terror as he tried to avoid them in the darkness.

Finally, at the age of 10, Michael was taken into care, but again found himself being consistently physically, sexually and emotionally abused. At the age of 14, he made the first of three unsuccessful suicide attempts. Long-serving staff at the children's home he was in have recently been convicted of abuse by the courts, though social workers at the time did not treat his allegations seriously. At the age of 15, Michael returned to his family home. He found work and spent most evenings out drinking so that he did not have to come into close contact with his family, particularly his mother and new stepfather, whom he strongly disliked. By this time, Michael was seriously disturbed and depressed and in a state of mind that he, his probation officer and one of his doctors all later considered had led to his commission of a violent offence. The doctor judged that the offence was a specific acting out of aggression against Michael's mother. Michael himself has now made a deliberate decision to cease contact with her. However, his renewal of contact with his father has finally helped him to understand the reasons why his father left, an act that devastated Michael for years and removed from him the protection of an adult he trusted. During his 15 years of incarceration there has been little sign of Michael receiving professional help to try to understand his violent behaviour and how he can avoid it in future. Instead, he has turned to religion and believes that this has expiated his feelings of anger. A final ingredient is that his newfound father is now dying of cancer.

Had the abuse of Michael, and others like him, been recognised and the child and his family managed differently as a result, it is possible that the long-term outcome, not just for him, but for many of these young men, might have been different. This is not to suggest that child abuse or loss are the only potential causes of violent offending, or that every abused child will offend, rather that abuse is sufficiently prevalent among such young people to be regarded as a key factor that responsible professionals should have in mind as they engage with children and young people, along the dichotomous welfare/justice continuum. Recurrently, research evidence such as the Edinburgh longitudinal study on youth transitions and crime (Smith and McVie, 2003) reminds us of the seemingly paradoxical but nevertheless close relationship between the young person's own victimisation at some point in their lives, and the offending.

Yule, in a critique of issues and findings relating to childhood abuse points out that '[o]ne reason why professionals did not believe that children were subject to physical or sexual abuse, or suffered from PTSD [post-traumatic stress disorder] was simply – that they never asked them!' (1993: 165). Yule's view confirmed an earlier study of 105 hospitalised psychiatric patients, which found that 51% of them had been sexually abused in childhood or adolescence, but that in the majority of these cases hospital staff were unaware of the abuse (Craine et al, 1988). Further, only 20% of the abused patients believed that they had received adequate treatment for their abusive experiences. These findings show quite clearly the need for involved professionals to inform themselves about the signs of abuse and the research findings that link abuse and later problems such as violence and mental illness.

Implications for a balanced approach

This chapter has concentrated deliberately on the cultural legitimacy afforded to violence to children across the world, and on the prevalence of abuse and loss in the childhoods of young people who offend violently, which is to be found in 'dangerous' young people across the age spectrum. It is not suggested here that this is the whole story. There are other factors that may influence and combine to precipitate violent acts. The ingredients discussed above are, however, too often overlooked not just by the general public, but also by criminal justice professionals. The youth offending, probation and prison services are increasingly exhorted to concentrate on more immediate 'criminogenic need', leading potentially to the neglect of earlier life events which may, on the face of it, seem unconnected but, with sustained investigation, may prove to be more criminogenic than any peer group pressure or substance addiction.

The foregoing discussion highlights a number of prevention issues: the need for more effective mechanisms to enable victims to report abuse; the assessment and intervention requirements for a comprehensive understanding of the dynamics of abuse and traumatic loss; and the necessity of supplementing existing gaps in knowledge about the variables that intervene either to prevent or exacerbate the likelihood of violent offending. The criminal justice services, in their crime prevention and multi-agency collaboration roles, could very importantly consider their contribution in these fields to the long-term reduction of victims who may later become perpetrators. A responsible use of the knowledge base described herein, for example, would be a pre-sentence examination of known background factors in violent offending, which is clearly linked to sentencing proposals addressing and seeking to eradicate these factors, while providing an acceptable level of protection for the public. The Riyadh Guidelines for the Prevention of Juvenile Delinquency state that custody should only be used as a last resort (UN, 1990). Where secure containment is necessary for public protection, however, proper provision should be made for interventions such as counselling following child abuse and other background traumata. Such practice would require that professionals familiarise themselves with the features of such traumata, such as post-traumatic stress disorder (PTSD) (Scott and Stradling, 1992; Dyregrov and Yule, 2006), so that when, for example, a youngster starts to tell them about recurrent nightmares or flashbacks, they recognise these as symptoms of PTSD and, rather than let it pass, pursue it via sensitive questioning.

There is, however, a final message for those called upon to work with young people who, for whatever reason, have become labelled as 'dangerous'. Assessing and managing dangerousness has become a challenging and high-profile task. It is not, by any means, impossible but it should be approached with careful consideration of significant ingredients that often lie hidden and upon which research findings beyond the 'What Works?' orthodoxy may well be able to throw light. In employing such an approach, practitioners not only afford greater protection to the public through being able to address these ingredients, but also provide the young people themselves with a long overdue 'good authority' (Pitt-Aikens and Thomas Ellis, 1990), within which their own victim experiences may finally be heard within a climate of compassion and understanding.

'Getting tough' is a short-term measure that solves nothing. 'Being effective' is recognising the complex links in the chain to youth violence and doing something about them both before and after they manifest themselves. However, as Gelsthorpe (2006: 424) has recently observed in respect of women and the criminal justice system, '[w]e've said it before, but we seem to have to say it again and again and again'.

An integrated response to young people classed as 'dangerous' through a research-based pinpointing of prevention, assessment and intervention techniques relevant to the complexities of contemporary social culture would perform a major service to victims and young people alike. However, interaction with local communities is also of the essence. The public is justifiably concerned about such young people; its protection may better be served through straightforward explanatory dialogue and guidance than by some imagined fail-safe surveillance system. Justice for individuals and communities alike will only be served by developing a shared understanding of the ingredients that pervade this elusive construct known as 'dangerousness'.

References

American Psychiatric Association (2000) *Diagnostic and statistical manual of mental disorders* (DSM-IV R), 5th edn, Washington, DC: American Psychiatric Association.

Bailey, S. (1996) 'Adolescents who murder', *Journal of Adolescence*, vol 19, no 1, pp 19–39.

Bichard, Sir Michael (2004) *An independent inquiry arising from the Soham murders*, London: The Stationery Office.

Blom-Cooper, L. (1985) *A child in trust: The report of the panel of inquiry into the circumstances surrounding the death of Jasmine Beckford*, Wembley: London Borough of Brent.

Boswell, G.R. (1995) *Violent victims*, London: The Prince's Trust.

Boswell, G.R. (1996) *Young and dangerous: The backgrounds and careers of section 53 offenders*, Aldershot: Avebury.

Bowling, B. (1998) *Violent racism: Victimisation, policing and social context*, Oxford: Clarendon Press.

Bureau of International Labour Affairs (1996) *Forced labor: The prostitution of children*, Washington, DC: US Department of Labor.

Bureau of International Labor Affairs (1998) *By the sweat and toil of children*, Washington, DC: US Department of Labor.

Bureau of International Labor Affairs (2006) *The Department of Labor's 2005 findings on the worst forms of child labor*, Washington, DC: US Department of Labor.

Butler-Sloss, Dame Elizabeth (1988) *Report of the inquiry into child abuse in Cleveland 1987*, London: HMSO.

Calouste Gulbenkian Foundation (1995) *Children and violence*, London: Calouste Gulbenkian Foundation.

Clancy, A., Hough, M., Aust, R. and Kershaw, C. (2001) *Crime, policing and justice: The experience of ethnic minorities: Findings from the 2000 British Crime Survey*, Home Office Research Study no 223, London: Home Office.

Craine, L.S., Henson, C.E., Colliver, J.A. and Maclean, D.G. (1988) 'Prevalence of a history of sexual abuse among female psychiatric patients in a state hospital system', *Hospital and Community Psychiatry*, vol 39, no 3, pp 300–4.

Creighton, S.J. (2004) *Prevalence and incidence of child abuse: International comparisons*, NSPCC Inform, London: NSPCC.

Creighton, S.J. and Tissier, G. (2003) *Child killings in England and Wales*, NSPCC Inform, London: NSPCC.

Dyregrov, A. and Yule, W. (2006) 'A review of PTSD in children', *Child and Adolescent Mental Health*, vol 11, no 4, pp 176–84.

Falshaw, L. (2005) 'The link between a history of maltreatment and subsequent offending behaviour', *Probation Journal,* vol 52, no 4, pp 423–34.

Falshaw, L. and Browne, K. (1997) 'Adverse childhood experiences and violent acts of young people in secure accommodation', *Journal of Mental Health*, vol 6, no 5, pp 443–56.

Garland, J. and Chakraborti, N. (2004) 'Racist victimisation, community safety and the rural: Issues and challenges', *British Journal of Community Justice*, vol 2, no 3, pp 21–32.

Garside, R. (2006) *Right for the wrong reasons: Making sense of criminal justice failure*, London: Crime and Society Foundation.

Gelles, R.J. and Straus, M.A. (1988) *Intimate violence*, New York: Simon and Schuster.

Gelsthorpe, L. (2006) 'Women and criminal justice: Saying it again, again and again', *Howard Journal of Criminal Justice*, vol 45, no 4, pp 421–24.

Goldson, B. (2002) *Vulnerable inside: Children in secure and penal settings,* London: The Children's Society.

Goldson, B. (2006) 'Damage, harm and death in child prisons in England and Wales: Questions of abuse and accountability', *Howard Journal of Criminal Justice*, vol 45, no 5, pp 449–67.

Hamilton, C.E., Falshaw, L. and Browne, K.D. (2002) 'The link between recurrent maltreatment and offending behaviour', *International Journal of Offender Therapy and Comparative Criminology*, vol 46, no 1, pp 75–94.

Hedderman, C. and Hough, M. (2004) 'Getting tough or being effective: What matters?', in G. Mair (ed), *What matters in probation*, Cullompton: Willan Publishing, pp 146-69.

Home Office, Lord Chancellor's Department and Attorney-General (2002) *Justice for all*, Cm 5563, London: The Stationery Office.

John, M. (2003) *Children's rights and power: Charging up for a new century*, London: Jessica Kingsley Publishers.

Laming, H. (2003) *The Victoria Climbié Inquiry: Report of an inquiry by Lord Laming, presented to Parliament by the Secretary of State for Health and the Secretary of State for the Home Department*, London: The Stationery Office.

Little, L. (2004) 'Victimisation of children with disabilities', in A. Kendall-Tackett (ed), *Health consequences of abuse in the family: A clinical guide for evidence-based practice*, Washington DC: American Psychological Association, pp 95-108.

Lösel, F. and Bender, D. (2006) 'Risk factors for serious and violent antisocial behaviour in children and youth', in A. Hagell and R. Jeyarajah-Dent (eds), *Children who commit acts of serious interpersonal violence: Messages for best practice*, London: Jessica Kingsley Publishers.

Midlands Probation Training Consortium (MPTC) in collaboration with Midlands Region Association of Chief Probation Officers (1998) *From murmur to murder: Working with racist offenders*, Birmingham: MPTC.

Pitt-Aikens, T. and Thomas Ellis, A. (1990) *Loss of the good authority*, London and New York: Penguin.

Scott, M.J. and Stradling, S.G. (1992) *Counselling for post traumatic stress disorder*, Counselling in Practice Series, London, Newbury Park and New Delhi: Sage.

Smith, D. and McVie, S. (2003) 'Theory and method in the Edinburgh study of youth transitions and crime', *British Journal of Criminology*, vol 43, no 1, pp 169–95.

Taylor, M. and Quayle, E. (2003) *Child pornography: An internet crime*, Hove: Brunner-Routledge.

United Nations (1990) *Guidelines for the prevention of juvenile delinquency (The Riyadh Guidelines)*, New York: Department of Public Information.

United Nations General Assembly (1989) *Convention on the rights of the child*, New York: United Nations.

United Nations Secretary-General (2006) *World report on violence against children*, Geneva: UN Publishing Services.

Vizard, E. (2006) 'Children with sexually abusive behaviour: A special subgroup', in A. Hagell and R. Jeyarajah-Dent (eds), *Children who commit acts of serious interpersonal violence: Messages for best practice*, London: Jessica Kingsley Publishers, pp 73-91.

Wedge, P., Boswell, G., Dissel, A. (2000) 'Violent victims in South Africa: Key factors in the backgrounds of young, serious offenders', *Acta Criminologica*, vol 13, no 1, p 16, and vol 13, no 2, p 31-8.

Widom, C. and White, H. (1997) 'Problem behaviour in abused and neglected children grown up: Prevalence and co-occurrence of substance abuse, crime and violence', *Criminal Behaviour and Mental Health*, vol 7, no 4, pp 287–310.

Williams, B. and Canton, R. (2005) 'Victims of crime, offenders and communities', *British Journal of Community Justice*, vol 3, no 2, pp 1–8.

Yule, W. (1993) 'Children as victims and survivors', in P.J. Taylor (ed), *Violence in Society*, London: Royal College of Physicians.

Zwane, W. (2000) *Understanding children and youth: Pathways to a violent lifestyle – The South African case*, Johannesburg: Centre for the Study of Violence and Reconciliation.

Mental health, risk and antisocial behaviour in young offenders: challenges and opportunities

4

Sue Bailey, Robert Vermeiren and Paul Mitchell

Introduction

There is a significant overlap between the risk factors for offending, poor mental health and substance misuse and the number of assessed risk factors increases as a young person moves further into the youth justice system (Youth Justice Board, 2005b).

For several reasons, high rates of mental disorders may be expected in young people in contact with youth justice services. First, prevalence rates of psychiatric disorders in community samples were shown to be around 15% (Roberts et al, 1998). Also, severe delinquency is common in the adolescent population, with about 5% showing an early onset and persistent pattern of antisocial behaviour (Moffitt, 1993). A substantial number of adolescents will show offending behaviour and will have a mental health disorder simply because of coincidental overlap between both conditions. Second, because offending and antisocial behaviour reaches high levels among youth justice populations, a diagnosis of conduct disorder (CD) will often be made. Because CD shows high co-morbidity rates with several other psychiatric disorders (Angold et al, 1999), increased levels of many types of disorder may be expected. Third, risk factors for youthful offending overlap substantially with those for several types of non-disruptive child psychiatric disorders, therefore identical risk factors may underlie both antisocial behaviour and emotional or developmental problems. Finally, selection processes may play a role. Disorders for which mental health interventions are provided, such as substance-use disorders (SUDs), may also lead to judicial involvement. Also, because of the prevalence of complex co-morbidity, treatment in a regular mental health care programme may be intricate and often is not possible, thus increasing the likelihood of judicial involvement. In addition, severely disordered persons may be less likely to have the personal capability and adequate resources to defend themselves and to avoid more drastic legal interventions.

Over the last 10 years, advances in developmental psychopathology and increased understanding of the continuities between child and adult life (Maughan and Kim-Cohen, 2005) have served as a timely reminder that many childhood disorders, once thought to resolve with age, are known to cast long shadows over later development.

Prevalence and meeting needs

Research on the prevalence of mental disorders in youth justice has increased steadily during the past years but remains limited compared with similar research in adults. There are a number of limitations to the research including: variations in the type and nature of psychiatric interviews by study, differences in the period of diagnostic assessment used in studies, differences in relevant sociodemographic and criminological characteristics, a focus in some studies on antisocial youths referred specifically for psychiatric assessment that limits the potential to generalise findings towards the whole youth offending population, and a lack of information from parents which may hamper the reliability of findings.

Although research consistently reveals high levels of psychiatric disorders among detained young people, rates vary widely by study, ranging from more than 50% to 100% (Atkins et al, 1999; Teplin et al, 2002; Vermeiren et al, 2002; Dixon et al, 2004; Lederman et al, 2004). CD and SUDs carry highest prevalence rates, but other mental disorders also present commonly in this population.

There is a high prevalence of mental health problems among young people in custody. Research published in 2005 (using a sample drawn from both community and secure settings) revealed the following mental health issues for young people who offend:

- 31% have mental health problems;
- 18% had problems with depression;
- 10% suffer from anxiety;
- 9% report a history of self-harm in the preceding month;
- 9% suffer from post-traumatic stress disorder;
- 7% have problems with hyperactivity;
- 5% report psychotic-like symptoms (Youth Justice Board, 2005a).

One in five young people were identified as having mental retardation (IQ<70). Additionally, unmet needs were identified across education as 48% and social relationships 36%. Needs were unmet because they were not recognised.

Decades of scientific research on the phenomenon of adolescent antisocial behaviour have resulted in the recognition of a large number of environmental and individual risk factors (Rutter et al, 1998). Until recently, research on psychiatric pathology as risk factors for offending has not received much attention and has therefore remained a subject of ongoing scientific debate (Vermeiren, 2003), although interest in the subject seems to have grown over recent years. As the current research has consistently shown high rates of disorders, the debate is slowly shifting towards aspects of clinical relevance (such as for judicial handling and therapeutic intervention). For specific disorders with overall low prevalence, such as autism-spectrum disorders and psychosis, research is still on the epidemiological level.

Progress has also been made in both the development of validated screening and need and risk assessment tools for this specific population (Grisso et al, 2005; Bailey et al, 2006; Bailey and Tarbuck, 2006) and in the development of promising interventions (Harrington and Bailey, 2004; Bailey and Williams, 2005).

Child and adolescent mental health practitioners have the skills to set the understanding of offending in a developmental context and treat those young people with mental disorders (Bailey, 2006). However, too often, mental health treatment within the youth justice system is lacking for those in need. A study by Domalanta et al (2003) showed that only about 20% of depressed incarcerated youth and only 10% of adolescents with other disorders were receiving treatment. Fewer than half of incarcerated youth who required treatment because of SUDs received intervention (Johnson et al, 2004). For those reasons, it is necessary to conduct further research not only on the prevalence of mental health disorders but also on the related needs for intervention.

General principles of assessment

Standard clinical assessment tools used in child and adolescent psychiatry cover many of the areas considered in forensic child and adolescent risk assessments (Gowers, 2001). This is especially important as youth justice systems in particular are not always equitable. In choosing between the many scales available, it is important to question not just their proven scientific properties but also their feasibility for use by practitioners.

It is important to consider the purpose for which the scale is to be used (see Table 4.1). Scales that measure psychopathology may not be good ways of assessing the risk that the psychopathology poses. Measures used to map out types of symptom must have good content validity. An instrument required to pick out one group of symptomatic people from the rest of the community (for example, mental health screening of young people in custody) needs to have good criterion validity. A related issue is the extent to which the scale is intended to measure change.

Table 4.1: Assessment required (yes/no)

Purpose of assessment	Psychopathology	Need	Risk
Screening of all young people coming into contact with an agency			
Detailed assessment, for example for sentencing, planning treatment			
Measuring change, for example during treatment or sentence			

Needs assessment

Needs and risk assessment are two separate but intertwined processes. Assessment of danger to others and the need to address this problem is at the centre of legislative and policy decision making. Risk assessment has a theory and methodology separate from needs assessment. It combines statistical data with clinical information in a way that integrates historical variables, current crucial variables and the contextual or environmental factors. Some of these clinical and contextual factors are potential areas of need. Therefore needs assessment may both inform and be a response to the risk assessment process (see Figure 4.1) (Bailey, 2002; Bailey and Dolan, 2004). The reciprocal process can be termed 'risk management' when accurate information about the risk assessment, combined with recurrent needs assessment, leads to risk management procedures. A recurrent needs assessment and risk assessment process should identify changes in problem areas, thus leading to monitoring or intervention as part of risk management. Core to this assessment are appropriate mental health screening tools and processes that are available to the young person at any point in the system (Bailey and Tarbuck, 2006).

Needs assessment may have advantages over more traditional ways of diagnosing disorders, mainly because this method also indicates whether specific conditions need attention and intervention. A health care need should be distinguished from a general need. One definition of a health care need is a cardinal (significant) problem that can benefit from an intervention that is not being offered (Marshall et al, 1995). Other definitions focus on who makes the judgement of need. Researchers have refined both individual and population needs assessment methods to take into account the different perspectives of clients, caregivers and professionals (Marshall, 1994; Phelan et al, 1995; Kurtz et al, 1997).

Figure 4.1: Relationship between various screening, needs assessment, risk assessment and management approaches in juvenile justice systems

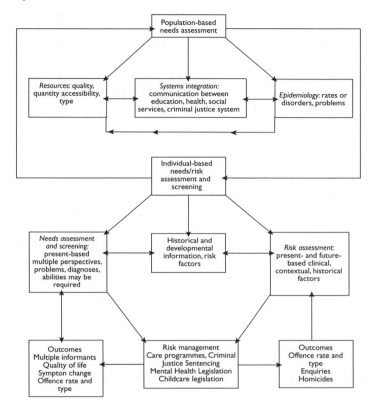

Source: Kroll, 2004

Risk assessment

The totality of the evidence base of risk factors for violent and antisocial behaviour has been used to develop structured risk assessment instruments that aim to increase the validity of clinical prediction. These scales typically contain a number of risk items selected from reviews of research, crime theories and clinical considerations (Farrington and Tarling, 1985; Le Blanc, 1998). Instruments vary with respect to the age and gender of their clients, problem intensity in the target groups, theoretical and empirical foundations, the number and domains of risks included, scoring procedures, time required for assessment, information sources, institutional contexts of administration and other issues (for example Hoge and Andrews, 1996; Le Blanc, 2002). Many instruments have been designed for application in youth justice systems (for example Hoge et al, 1996; Barnoski, 2002;

Borum et al, 2002), most of which contain factors from various areas of risk (for example individual, family, neighbourhood).

Risk assessment instruments need to comply with a number of methodological and practical criteria. Item content and scoring must be explicit in order to meet standards of objectivity and reliability. Systematic training should precede the application of a complex scale. Instruments must maintain a balance between broadness of information and economy. When screening large groups, it is best to apply a stepwise gating procedure (Loeber et al, 1984). Items should refer to multiple contexts of behaviour and use multiple sources of independent information (Achenbach et al, 1987; Losel and Beelmann, 2005). They should tap into not only static risks but also dynamic factors that can be changed by interventions. Information on risks should be complemented by data on protective factors and strengths; however, this is rarely the case (for example Borum et al, 2002). Although scales need to be sufficiently specific to target the child's age and gender, they should also enable systematic comparison across groups and time. In many countries, cultural differences will need to be taken into account (Cooke and Michie, 2001). Legal and ethical aspects also need to be integrated in order to avoid stigmatisation, violations of data protection and other problems (Le Blanc, 1998). Last, but not least, instruments need to be backed up with ongoing research on their validity (see section below on 'Psychopathic personality' in young people).

Mental disorders and offending

A developmental approach to violence, hostile attributions, paranoid thinking in adolescence

Bentall et al (1994) describe evidence from the adult literature that suggests three broad types of mechanisms that might be involved in delusional thinking in general, and paranoia in particular. These are anomalous perceptual experiences, abnormal reasoning and motivational factors.

Over the same timespan the focus in the field of child and adolescent mental health has been on:

*   developmental psychopathology in child and adolescent psychiatry and psychology;
*   the emphasis on hostile attribution and bias in understanding the aetiology of violent behaviour in young people and subsequent implications for psychological treatment interventions;
*   developing concepts linking attachment, theory of mind, mentalisation and impact of failed mentalisation on the evolution of violent behaviour in adolescence.

Fonagy (2003) has distilled out historical psychodynamic thinking, now supported by modern developmental data, to remind us that aggression and violence appear to be present from early childhood, toddlerhood and perhaps from birth. The concept here is that violence ultimately signals the failure of normal developmental processes to deal with something that occurs naturally. He explores the concept that violence is unlearned not learned, the role of disrupted insecure attachment in this process and the impact of failure of mentalisation in childhood.

Physical aggression peaks at around the second year of life and subsequently shows distinct developmental trajectories (Nagin and Tremblay, 2001; Shaw et al, 2003). Attachment enables the mastery of aggression, self-control being developed through the efficient exercise of attritional mechanisms and symbolisation. Fonagy et al (2002) have developed the concept of mentalisation, the capacity to understand others' subjective experience (Tomasello, 1999), and Fonagy (2003) also explores the biological evidence to link violence with impaired mentalisation, with the primary developmental role of early attachment being seen as neurocognitive in function.

Differences in language capability between violent and non-violent individuals reflect difference in the quality of early relationships rather than constitutional determinants restricted to language capacity. Early relationships are there not to simply protect the vulnerable infant but to organise the functioning of the brain, to create an environment in which a capacity for self-mastery can be achieved by creating a representational structure for mental status. Threats to self-esteem trigger violence in individuals whose self-appraisal is 'on shaky ground' and are unable to see behind the threats to what is in the mind of the person threatening them. These processes are played out in the complex and toxic co-morbidities seen so much more frequently in child and adolescent than in adult mental health practice.

Oppositional disorders, conduct disorder and ADHD

Substantially higher rates of physically aggressive behaviour are found in children and adolescents with attention-deficit hyperactivity disorder (ADHD), with those who meet the criteria for ADHD and conduct disorder having substantially greater risks of antisocial acts in adolescence, harmful acts in later adolescence and continued violence and offending into adulthood (Fischer et al, 1993; Frick, 1998a and 1998b). Children with hyperactivity, impulsivity, attention deficits and serious conduct problems may also be at risk of developing psychopathy (Seagrave and Grisso, 2002).

Distorted or biased thought processes have over time been implicated in the development of violence. Tenets central to psychological treatments aimed at reducing violent behaviour in adolescents and young adults traditionally centre on violence as learned behaviour and the idea that patterns of violence and criminal behaviour are embedded in habits of thinking (McGuire and Priestley, 1995). Significant cognitive attributional bias has been shown in aggressive children and young people. They are more likely to perceive neutral acts by others as hostile, and more likely to believe conflicts can be satisfactorily resolved by aggression. In the social context, as the young individual becomes more disliked and rejected by peers, the opportunity for viewing the world this way increases (Dodge and Schwartz, 1997). By their late teens they can hold highly suspicious attitudes and be quick to perceive disrespect from others. In the social context of juvenile incarceration, being 'para' (paranoid) can become the shared norm in peer group interactions (Farrant, 2001).

Depression anxiety and PTSD in childhood and adolescence

As well as the recognised feelings of low mood in depression there is also some evidence of irritability, hostility and anger when depression occurs in adolescence. Irritability in adolescence leads to interpreting annoyances by others as direct threats, increasing the risk of defensive aggression (Dubicka and Harrington, 2004). Nowhere is this more apparent than in youth justice populations (Kroll et al, 2002; Harrington et al, 2005). A self-serving bias with a tendency to attribute good outcomes to the self and bad outcomes to external causes observed in ordinary people is usually regarded as a mechanism for maintaining self-esteem in the face of threats to the self.

PTSD is related to the conditioning of neurobiological fear responses underlying tendencies to react aggressively to protect the self when exposed to reminders of earlier trauma (Fletcher, 2003). In the recent escalating context of children who have experienced violence in war-torn countries and those who live in a context of 'urban war zones', Garbarino (2001) sets out an ecological framework to explain the process and conditions that transform the 'developmental challenge' of violence into developmental harm in some children, an accumulation of risk model for understanding how and when children suffer the most adverse consequences of exposure to community violence and go beyond their limits of resilience, incorporating the concepts of 'social maps' as products of childhood experiences and of trauma as a psychological wound.

The combination of depression, anxiety and severe PTSD is being increasingly recognised in the literature on children as being linked to a trajectory into adult antisocial personality disorder (Harrington and Bailey, 2004).

Autism-spectrum disorders and learning disability

Autism-spectrum disorders are being increasingly recognised in adolescent forensic populations. Their identification is critical to the understanding of violent offending. This is particularly so if an offence or assault is bizarre in nature, the degree or nature of aggression is unaccountable and/or there is a stereotypical pattern of offending. O'Brien (1996) and Howlin (1997) proposed four reasons for offending and aggression in autistic persons:

- Their social naivety may allow them to be led into criminal acts by others.
- Aggression may arise from a disruption of routines.
- Antisocial behaviour may stem from a lack of understanding or misinterpretation of social cues.
- Crimes may reflect obsessions, especially when these involved morbid fascination with violence – there are similarities with the intense and obsessional nature of fantasies described in some adult sadists.

In the extant adult research on paranoid beliefs and autism-spectrum disorder, authors such as Craig et al (2004) and Blackshaw et al (2001) conclude from utilising measures of Theory of Mind that 'the paranoia observed in Asperger's syndrome does not appear to stem from the same factors as seen in the paranoia observed in people with a diagnosis of schizophrenia' (Blackshaw et al, 2001: 158). They postulate that the paranoia in the former has a different quality to that observed in the latter. Rather than stemming from a defensive strategy, it may stem from a confusion of not understanding the subtleties of social interaction and social rules. In this case there are no reasons for those with Asperger's syndrome to make abnormal attributions.

Early-onset psychosis

Non-psychotic behavioural disturbance occurs in about half of cases of early-onset schizophrenia and can last between one and seven years. It includes externalising behaviours, attention-deficit disorder and conduct disorder. This emphasises the need for mental health assessments repeated over time to include a focus on changes in social functioning (often from an already chaotic baseline level) to a state including perceptual distortion, ideas of reference and delusional mood (Clark, 2001).

The same as is the case for adults (Taylor and Gunn, 1999), most young people with schizophrenia are non-delinquent and non-violent. Nevertheless, there may be an increased risk of violence to others when they have active symptoms, especially when there is misuse of drugs or alcohol. The risk of violent acts is related to subjective feelings of tension, ideas of violence, delusional symptoms that incorporate named persons known to the individual, persecutory delusions, fear of imminent attack, feelings of sustained anger and fear, passivity experiences reducing the sense of self-control and command hallucinations. Protective factors include responding to and compliance with physical and psychosocial treatments, good social networks, a valued home environment, no interest in or knowledge of weapons as a means of violence, good insight into the psychiatric illness and any previous violent aggressive behaviour and a fear of their own potential for violence. These features require particular attention but the best predictors of future violent offending in young people with mental disorder are the same as those in the general adolescent population (Clare et al, 2000). In findings from a retrospective study of 39 young people aged from 12 to 18 admitted to a specialist national medium-secure inpatient adolescent unit and a regional adolescent inpatient unit, Clare et al (2000) found that the violence was related to developmental and social factors rather than psychopathology, which included persecutory delusions present in 12 of the 14 in the violent group and 23 of the 25 in the non-violent group.

'Psychopathic personality' in young people

A three-factor structure has been proposed (Cooke and Michie, 2001), which includes:

- an arrogant, deceitful interpersonal style, involving dishonesty, manipulation, grandiosity and glibness;
- defective emotional experience, involving lack of remorse, poor empathy, shallow emotions and a lack of responsibility for one's own actions;
- behavioural manifestations of impulsiveness, irresponsibility and sensation seeking.

Conduct disorder, antisocial personality disorder and psychopathy are often seen as developmental disorders that span the life course and the terms are sometimes used interchangeably. Conduct disorder and antisocial personality disorder primarily focus on behavioural problems whereas psychopathy, as described by Hare (1991), emphasises deficits in affective and interpersonal functioning.

A consensus is likely to be reached only when we have longitudinal studies demonstrating the stability of psychopathic traits over the lifespan and evidence that the same aetiological factors contribute to this disorder at all ages. As there is significant overlap between the behavioural aspects of youth psychopathy and ADHD and between the callous-unemotional dimension of psychopathy and autistic-spectrum disorders, future work needs to disentangle these constructs from a phenomenological and aetiological perspective. As yet, there are few studies of the outcome of treatment for young people with psychopathic traits, although the limited data suggest that these traits might be a moderator of outcome. Most clinicians view youth psychopathy as a potentially treatable disorder and there is some evidence that identification of psychopathic traits in young people has a number of benefits, which include:

- identifying young people who offend who pose a high risk;
- reducing misclassifications that have negative ramifications for children and adolescents;
- improving and optimising treatment planning for young people with psychopathic traits who may require more intensive and risk-focused therapeutic approaches.

Substance misuse

The relationship between substance misuse, and more specifically cannabis use, and the development of schizophrenia and other psychoses has been well established (Rey and Tennant, 2002; Green et al, 2005; Semple et al, 2005), although recent research has implied either a common vulnerability or bidirectional causal relationship between the use of cannabis and psychosis (Ferdinand et al, 2005). The correlation between the self-reported drug use and the onset of schizophrenia differs significantly from the correlation with affective disorders and non-schizophrenic, non-affective disorders (Weiser et al, 2003). In comparing psychiatric outcomes at age 26 with the use of cannabis during adolescence, Arseneault et al (2002) added to the current evidence base with three new findings. The authors found that cannabis use is associated with an increased risk of experiencing symptoms of schizophrenia. After controlling for those symptoms that precede the onset of cannabis use, the onset of cannabis use before the age of 16 increases the risk of such symptoms developing and this risk is specific to cannabis use. In a prospective cohort study (2,437 young people aged 14 to 24 years) of cannabis use, predisposition for psychosis and psychotic symptoms in young people, Henquet et al (2005) demonstrated that cannabis use moderately increases the risk of psychotic symptoms in young people but has a much stronger effect in those with evidence of predisposition for psychosis.

Working with young people with mental health problems: some practice points for interventions

Interventions with young people who offend, regardless of whether they are addressing offending behaviour or mental health problems, should take into account developmental and cognitive factors significant to this age group. Interventions designed for use with adults are usually highly structured and target driven. This style of intervention is often perceived by young people as alienating and not relevant to their lives with the result that they are likely to disengage (either actively or passively) from the programme.

The skills required to engage a young person in a 'therapeutic alliance' are often different to those necessary with adults who offend. Adult are more likely to see the value of participating in an enhanced thinking-skills course, possibly as a means to an early release or to improve the quality of relationships within their family unit. Such goals may be perceived as too long range to have any meaning to a young person, or simply seem irrelevant. Young people's general experience of relationships with adults, particularly professionals, is of authority figures that give instructions, set limits on behaviour, and, at best, are givers of information. The typical responses to this are to adopt an aggressive posture or one of passive indifference. To engage actively with young people who offend, professionals need to listen attentively and show interest in the young person's perspective. This does not mean agreeing with the young person's point of view; however, it is an opportunity to establish the 'middle ground' within which a therapeutic alliance may be fostered.

Adolescents who offend have often experienced unstable lives with disrupted attachments. Thus they often have difficulty in understanding the significance of life events such as trauma and bereavement that an adult will readily understand as likely to impact on emotional well-being. A thorough assessment prior to commencing an intervention and drawing on material from multiple sources, particularly parents or professionals who have a detailed knowledge of the young person, is very helpful. Events such as the loss of a parent and the onset of conduct problems are often closely linked temporally, yet young people frequently do not see any connection between such events.

A formulation is a brief statement that summarises the possible links between different aspects of the young person's life, for instance between a bereavement and the onset of behavioural difficulties. Young people who offend are often unable to make formulations because of their failure to understand how different elements of their lives are connected. The ability to make formulations can be seen as a developmental milestone and adolescents, for the reasons identified above, often lag behind their own peer group as well as the adult population. Regardless of whether addressing offending behaviours or mental health problems, professionals working with young people need to generate such formulations collaboratively so that they make sense both within the therapeutic framework and also within the young person's life experience.

Establishing therapeutic goals also needs to be done in a way that is collaborative and developmentally appropriate. Adolescence in general is characterised as a time of heightened emotional responses (partly as a result of hormonal changes), a growing but still limited capacity for problem solving and the tendency to seek immediate advantage rather than long-term gain. All of these factors are likely to be enhanced in young people who offend in contrast with the rest of their peer group. Goal setting therefore needs to concentrate heavily on the short term, namely within the young person's perceived time frame. Targets and rewards should be low-key in order to reduce the likelihood of extreme emotional responses to success or failure. Therapists working with young people need to be active in encouraging the generation of alternative solutions in order to extend the young person's range of problem-solving skills.

Young people's capacity to generate alternative strategies is often restricted by their own, limited emotional range. They will typically respond to any adverse event with hostility and anger, events that would typically evoke a response of sadness or fear within adults. Work on emotional recognition with young people who offend will assist them in recognising a wider range of emotions, both in themselves and others. This enhances their range of options when faced with future adverse events.

There is often a tendency to concentrate on behavioural objectives as the most easily recognised or measured outcomes. However, working on goals such as recognising and managing arousal levels, or shifting cognitions or attributions in specific situations may prove more beneficial in the longer term even if immediate behavioural changes are not achieved.

Goal setting and intervention strategies should be individually tailored and take into account differences in cognitive ability, maturity and insight within this population. To ensure that the young person remains actively engaged in the intervention process it is important to check their perception of how effective the therapy is frequently, and whether the goals and strategies are relevant. Therapists should often check the young person's level of understanding to ensure that the communication is two-way and repeats elements or themes as necessary to ensure good compliance and comprehension, rather than adhering to a timetable.

Conclusion

Standard 9 (the CAMHS standard) of the Children's National Service Framework (NSF) for Children, Young People and Maternity Services (Department of Health, 2004) has set out a vision of a comprehensive child and adolescent mental health service. A young person in contact with the criminal justice system, whether in custody, or in the community, should have the same access to this comprehensive service as any other child or young person within the general population. Treatment options should not be affected by a young person's status within the criminal justice system. The NSF has established a clear responsibility for primary care trusts to ensure that local needs assessments identify young people in special circumstances, including young offender institutions, and sets out expectations that services are in place to meet their needs. It also states that all young people from birth to their 18th birthday should have access to timely, integrated services.

The major challenge of altering the trajectories of young people who offend persistently has to be met in the context of satisfying public demands for retribution, together with welfare and civil liberties considerations. Treatment of young people in institutional settings has to meet the sometimes contradictory need to control young people, to remove their liberty and to maintain good order in the institution, at the same time as offering education and training to foster future pro-social participation in society and meeting their welfare needs. At least in England and Wales, the legislative overhaul of youth justice (1998 Crime and Disorder Act) has mandated practitioners to bridge the gap between residential and community treatments and to involve families using Youth Offending Teams (YOTs) to meet this complex mix of needs, including mental health needs.

So, coming full circle, our knowledge of true prevalence rates of mental disorders in a young offending population is developing further (Kazdin, 2000) so that mental health issues can be addressed. Child and adolescent mental health practitioners have the skills to set the understanding of offending in a developmental context and treat those young people with mental disorders (Bailey, 2006).

What are the key levers for change? From a mental health perspective these include:

- developing an integrated comprehensive screening and assessment tool for mental health, substance misuse and physical health (work to be completed by the end of 2007);
- better identification of mental health needs by courts with effective court diversion;
- improving access to child and adolescent mental health services for 16 to 17 year olds across the board;
- enhancing the role of health workers in YOTs;
- integrating the work of substance misuse workers in custody and YOTs;
- enhancing intensive resettlement and aftercare provision – RAP schemes;
- reviewing the demand and need for nationally commissioned adolescent psychiatric secure inpatient beds;
- ensuring that all those working with young people understand and are trained in normal and abnormal child and adolescent development together with awareness of the nature of mental health problems in this stage of the life course and how this has an impact on all aspects of a young person's life.

References

Achenbach, T.M., McConaughy, S.H. and Howell, C.T. (1987) 'Child/adolescent behavioral and emotional problems: Implications of cross-informant correlations for situational specificity', *Psychological Bulletin*, vol 101, no 2, pp 213–32.

Angold, A., Costello, E.J. and Erkanli, A. (1999) 'Co-morbidity', *Journal of Child Psychology and Psychiatry*, vol 40, no 1, pp 57–87.

Arseneault, L., Cannon, M., Poulton, R., Murray, R., Caspi, A. and Moffitt, T.E. (2002) 'Cannabis use in adolescence and risk for adult psychosis: Longitudinal prospective study', *British Medical Journal*, vol 325, no 7374, pp 1212–1213.

Atkins, D., Pumariega, A.J., Rogers, K., Montgomery, L., Nybro, C., Jeffers, G. and Sease, F. (1999) 'Mental health and incarcerated youth: Prevalence and nature of psychopathology', *Journal of Child Family Studies*, vol 8, no 2, pp 193–204.

Bailey, S. (2002) 'Violent children: A framework for assessment', *Advances in Psychiatric Treatment*, vol 8, no 2, pp 97–106.

Bailey, S. (2006) 'Adolescence and beyond: Twelve years onwards', in J. Aldgate, W. Rose, D. Jones and C. Jeffrey (eds), *The developing world of the child: 12*, London: Jessica Kingsley Publishers, pp 208–25.

Bailey, S. and Dolan, M. (2004) 'Violence', in S. Bailey and M. Dolan (eds), *Adolescent forensic psychiatry*, London: Arnold Publishing, pp 213–27.

Bailey, S., Doreleijers, T. and Tarbuck, P. (2006) 'Recent developments in mental health screening and assessment in juvenile justice systems', *Psychiatric Clinics of North America*, vol 15, pp 391–406.

Bailey, S. and Tarbuck, P. (2006) 'Recent advances in the development of screening tools for mental health in young offenders', *Current Opinion in Psychiatry*, vol 19, no 4, pp 373–7.

Bailey, S. and Williams, R. (2005) 'Forensic mental health services for children and adolescents. AACAP Official Action', in R. Williams and M. Kerfoot (eds), *Child and adolescent mental health service, strategy, planning, delivery and evaluation 18*, Oxford: Oxford University Press, pp 271–95.

Barnoski, R. (2002) 'Monitoring vital signs: Integrating a standardized assessment into Washington State's juvenile justice system', in R. Corrado, R. Roesch, S. Hart and J.K. Gierowski (eds), *Multi-problem violent youth: A foundation for comparative research on needs, interventions and outcomes*, Amsterdam: IOS Press, pp 219–31.

Bentall, R., Kinderman, P. and Kaney, S. (1994) 'The self, attributional process and normal beliefs: Towards a model of persecutory delusions', *Behaviour Research and Therapy*, vol 32, no 3, pp 331–41.

Blackshaw, A.J., Kinderman, P., Hare, D.J. and Hatton, C. (2001) 'Theory of mind, causal attribution and paranoia in Asperger syndrome', *Autism*, vol 5, no 2, pp 147–63.

Borum, R., Bartel, P. and Forth, A. (2002) *Manual for the structured assessment of violence risk in youth (SAVRY)*, Tampa, FL: University of South Florida.

Clare, P., Bailey, S. and Clark, A. (2000) 'Relationship between psychotic disorders in adolescence and criminally violent behaviour', *British Journal of Psychiatry*, vol 177, no 3, pp 275–9.

Clark, R.E. (2001) 'Family support and substance use outcomes for persons with mental illness and substance use disorders', *Schizophrenia Bulletin*, vol 27, no 1, pp 93–101.

Cooke, D.J. and Michie, C. (2001) 'Refining the construct of psychopathy: Towards a hierarchical model', *Psychological Assessment*, vol 13, no 2, pp 171–88.

Craig, J., Hatton, C., Crain, F. and Bentall, R. (2004) 'Persecutory beliefs, attributions and theory of mind: Comparison of patients with paranoid delusions, Asperger's syndrome and healthy controls', *Schizophrenia Research*, vol 69, no 1, pp 29–3.

Department of Health (2004) *National service framework for children, young people and maternity services*, London: Department of Health.

Dixon, A., Howie, P. and Starling, J. (2004) 'Psychopathology in female offenders', *Journal of Child Psychology and Psychiatry*, vol 45, no 6, pp 1150–8.

Dodge, K.A. and Schwartz, D. (1997) 'Social information processing mechanisms in aggressive behavior', in D.M. Stoff, J. Breiling and J.D. Maser (eds), *Handbook of antisocial behavior*, New York: Wiley, pp 171-80

Domalanta, D.D., Risser, W.L., Roberts, R.E. and Risser, J.M.H. (2003) 'Prevalence of depression and other psychiatric disorders among incarcerated youths', *Journal of the American Academy of Child and Adolescent Psychiatry*, vol 42, no 4, pp 477–84.

Dubicka, B. and Harrington, R. (2004) 'Affective conduct disorder', in S. Bailey and M. Dolan (eds), *Adolescent Forensic Psychiatry 10*, London: Arnold Publishing, pp 124–43.

Farrant, F. (2001) *Troubled inside: Responding to the mental health needs of children and young people in prison*, London: Prison Reform Trust.

Farrington, D.P. and Tarling, R. (eds), (1985) *Prediction in criminology*, Albany, NY: State University of New York Press.

Ferdinand, R.F., Sondeijker, F., van der Ende, J., Selten J.P., Huizink, A. and Verhulst, F.C. (2005) 'Cannabis use predicts future psychotic symptoms, and vice versa', *Addiction*, vol 100, no 5, pp 612–18.

Fischer, M., Barkley, R.A., Fletcher, K.E. and Smallish, L. (1993) 'The adolescent outcome of hyperactive children: Predictors of psychiatric, academic, social and emotional adjustment', *Journal of the American Academy of Child and Adolescent Psychiatry*, vol 32, no 2, pp 324–32.

Fletcher, K.E. (2003) 'Childhood posttraumatic stress disorder', in E.J. Mash and R.A. Barkley (eds), *Child psychopathology*, 2nd edn, New York: Guildford Press, pp 330–71.

Fonagy, P., Target, M., Cottrell, D., Phillips, J. and Kurtz, Z. (2002) *What works for whom? A critical review of treatments for children and adolescents*, New York: Guilford Press.

Fonagy, P. (2003) 'Towards a developmental understanding of violence', *British Journal of Psychiatry*, vol 183, no 3, pp 190–2.

Frick, P.J. (1998a) 'Callous-unemotional traits and conduct problems: Applying the two-factor model of psychopathy to children', in D. Cooke, A. Forth and R. Hare (eds), *Psychopathy: Theory, research and implications for society*, Dordrecht: Kluwer, pp 161–89.

Frick, P.J. (1998b) *Conduct disorders and severe antisocial behaviour 2*, New York: Plenum Press.

Garbarino, J. (2001) 'An ecological perspective on the effects of violence on children', *Journal of Community Psychology*, vol 29, no 3, pp 361–78.

Gowers, S. (2001) 'Assessing adolescent mental health', in S. Gowers (ed), *Adolescent psychiatry in clinical practice*, London: Arnold Publishing, pp 258–77.

Green, B., Young, R. and Kavanagh, D. (2005) 'Cannabis use and misuse prevalence among people with psychosis', *British Journal of Psychiatry*, vol 187, no 4, pp 306–13.

Grisso, T., Vincent, G. and Seagrave, D. (eds), (2005) *Mental health screening and assessment in juvenile justice*, London: Guildford Press.

Hare, R.D. (1991) *The Hare psychopathy checklist – revised*, Toronto: Multi Health Systems.

Harrington, R.C. and Bailey, S. (2004) 'Prevention of antisocial personality disorder: Mounting evidence on optimal timing and methods (editorial)', *Criminal Behaviour and Mental Health*, vol 14, pp 75–81.

Harrington, R.C., Kroll, L., Rothwell, J., McCarthy, K., Bradley, D. and Bailey, S. (2005) 'Psychosocial needs of boys in secure care for serious or persistent offending', *Journal of Child Psychology and Psychiatry*, vol 46, no 8, pp 859–66.

Henquet, C., Krabbendam, L., Spauwen, J., Kaplan, C., Lieb, R., Wittchen, H.-U. and Van Os, J. (2005) 'Prospective cohort study of cannabis use, predisposition for psychosis, and psychotic symptoms in young people', *British Medical Journal*, vol 330, no 7481, pp 11–14.

Hoge, R.D. and Andrews, D.A. (1996) *Assessing the youthful offender: Issues and techniques*, New York: Plenum Press.

Hoge, R.D., Andrews, D.A. and Leschied, A.W. (1996) 'An investigation of risk and protective factors in a sample of youthful offenders', *Journal of Child Psychology and Psychiatry and Allied Disciplines*, vol 37, no 4, pp 419–24.

Howlin, P. (1997) *Autism: Preparing for adulthood*, London: Routledge.

Johnson, T.P., Cho, Y.I., Fendrich, M., Graf, I., Kelly-Wilson, L. and Pickup, L. (2004) 'Treatment need and utilisation among youth entering the juvenile corrections system', *Journal Substance Abuse Treatment*, vol 26, no 2, pp 117–28.

Kazdin, A.E. (2000) 'Adolescent development, mental disorders, and decision making of delinquent youths', in T. Grisso and R.G. Schwartz (eds), *Youth on Trial: A developmental perspective on juvenile justice 2*, Chicago: University of Chicago Press, pp 33–65.

Kroll, L. (2004) 'Needs assessment in adolescent offenders', in S. Bailey and M. Dolan (eds), *Adolescent forensic psychiatry*, London: Arnold Publishing, pp 14-26.

Kroll, L., Rothwell, J., Bradley, D., Shah, P., Bailey, S. and Harrington, R.C. (2002) 'Mental health needs of boys in secure care for serious or persistent offending: A prospective, longitudinal study', *The Lancet*, vol 359, no 9322, pp 1975–9.

Kurtz, Z., Thornes, R. and Bailey, S. (1997) 'Children in the criminal justice and secure care systems: How their mental health needs are met', *Journal of Adolescence*, vol 21, pp 543–53.

Le Blanc, M. (1998) 'Screening of serious and violent juvenile offenders: Identification, classification, and prediction', in R. Loeber and D. Farrington (eds), *Serious and violent juvenile offenders: Risk factors and successful interventions*, Thousand Oaks, CA: Sage Publications, pp 167–93.

Le Blanc, M. (2002) 'The offending cycle, escalation and de-escalation in delinquent behaviour: A challenge for criminology', *International Journal of Comparative and Applied Criminal Justice*, vol 26, no 1, pp 53–84.

Lederman, C.S., Dakof, G.A., Larrea, M.A. and Li, H. (2004) 'Characteristics of adolescent females in juvenile detention', *International Journal of Law and Psychiatry*, vol 27, no 4, pp 321–37.

Loeber, R., Dishion, T.J. and Patterson, G.R. (1984) 'Multiple gating: A multistage assessment procedure for identifying youths at risk for delinquency', *Journal of Research in Crime & Delinquency*, vol 21, no 1, pp 7–32.

Losel, F. and Beelmann, A. (2005) 'Social problem-solving programs for preventing antisocial behavior in children and youth', in M. McMurran and J. McGuire (eds), *Social problem solving and offending: Evidence, evaluation and evolution*, New York: John Wiley & Sons, pp 127–43.

McGuire, J. and Priestley, P. (1995) 'Reviewing "what works": Past present and future', in J. McGuire (ed), *What works: Reducing reoffending: Guidelines from research and practice*, Chichester: Wiley, pp 3–34.

Marshall, M. (1994) 'How should we measure need? Concept and practice in the development of a standardized assessment schedule', *Philosophy, Psychiatry and Pschology*, vol 1, no 1, pp 27–36.

Marshall, M., Hogg, L., Gath, D.H. and Lockwood, A. (1995) 'The cardinal needs schedule: A modified version of the MRC Needs for Care Assessment Schedule', *Psychological Medicine*, vol 25, no 3, pp 605–17.

Maughan, B. and Kim-Cohen, J. (2005) 'Continuities between childhood and adult life', *British Journal of Psychiatry*, vol 187, no 4, pp 301–3.

Moffitt, T.E. (1993) 'Adolescence – limited and life-course – persistent antisocial behaviour: Development taxonomy', *Psychology Review*, vol 100, pp 674–701.

Nagin, D. and Tremblay, R.E. (2001) 'Parental and early childhood predictors of persistent physical aggression in boys from kindergarten to high school', *Archives of General Psychiatry*, vol 58, no 4, pp 389–94.

O'Brien, G. (1996) 'The psychiatric management of adult autism', *Advances in Psychiatric Treatment*, vol 2, pp 173–7.

Phelan, M., Slade, M. and Thornicroft, G. (1995) 'The Camberwell Assessment Need (CAN): The viability and reliability of an instrument to assess the needs of people with severe mental illness', *British Journal of Psychiatry*, vol 167, no 4, pp 589–95.

Rey, J.M. and Tennant, C.C. (2002) 'Cannabis and mental health: More evidence establishes clear link between use of cannabis and psychiatric illness', *British Medical Journal*, vol 325, no 7374, pp 1183–4.

Roberts, R.E., Attkisson, C.C. and Roseblatt, A. (1998) 'Prevalence of psychopathology among children and adolescents', *American Journal of Psychiatry*, vol 155, no 6, pp 715–25.

Rutter, M., Giller, H. and Hagell, A. (1998) *Antisocial behavior by young people*, Cambridge: Cambridge University Press.

Seagrave, D. and Grisso, T. (2002) 'Adolescent development and the measurement of juvenile psychopathy', *Law and Human Behavior*, vol 26, no 2, pp 219–39.

Semple, D.M., McIntosh, A.M. and Lawrie, S.M. (2005) 'Cannabis as a risk factor for psychosis: Systematic review', *Journal of Psychopharmacology*, vol 19, no 2, pp 187–94.

Shaw, D.S., Gillion, M., Ingoldsby, E.M. and Nagin, D.S. (2003) 'Trajectories leading to school-age conduct problems', *Developmental Psychology*, vol 39, no 2, pp 189–200.

Taylor, P.J. and Gunn, J. (1999) 'Homicides by people with mental illness myth and reality', *British Journal of Psychiatry*, vol 174, no 1, pp 9–14.

Teplin, L.A., Abram, K.M., McClelland, G.M., Dulcan, M.K. and Mericle, A.A. (2002) 'Psychiatric disorders in youth in juvenile detention', *Archives of General Psychiatry*, vol 59, no 12, pp 1133–43.

Tomasello, M. (1999) 'The human adaptation for culture', *Annual Review of Anthropology*, vol 28, pp 509–29.

Vermeiren, R. (2003) 'Psychopathology and delinquency in adolescents: A descriptive and developmental perspective', *Clinical Psychology Review*, vol 23, no 2, pp 277–318.

Vermeiren, R., Schwab-Stone, M., Ruchkin, V., De Clippele, A. and Deboutte, D. (2002) 'Predicting recidivism in delinquent adolescents from psychological and psychiatric assessment', *Comprehensive Psychiatry*, vol 43, no 2, pp 142–9.

Weiser, M., Reichenberg, A., Rabinowitz, J., Kaplan, Z., Yasivizky, R., Mark, M., Knobler, H.Y., Nahon, D. and Davidson, M. (2003) 'Self-reported drug abuse in male adolescents with behavioural disturbances, and follow-up for future schizophrenia', *Biological Psychiatry*, vol 54, no 6, pp 655–60.

Youth Justice Board (2005a) *Mental health needs and effectiveness of provision for young offenders in custody and the community*, London: Youth Justice Board.

Youth Justice Board (2005b) *Risk and protective factors*, London: Youth Justice Board.

5

Serious incidents in the youth justice system: management and accountability

Maggie Blyth

Introduction

Public opinion tends consistently to overestimate the scale and trend in offending as recorded in official crime data. This applies as much to offending among young people as it does to offending among adults. Over the last decade, youth crime has become highly politicised, resulting in soaring custodial figures and increasingly tough posturing by ministers over approaches to dealing with young people who commit crime. It is well documented elsewhere that, despite a stable or downward trend in offending by young people according to official figures (Audit Commission, 2004), there is a widespread view among the public that children and young people are out of control and criminal behaviour is increasing (Hough and Roberts, 2004; see also Kemshall and Nash, Chapters 1 and 6 in this volume). Although some of this can be attributed to the fact that actual youth offending figures in terms of self-reporting may be higher (Home Office, 2006), a handful of cases in recent months have caused a moral outcry and public disturbance, leading to a perception that violent crime is out of control. Reinforcing this view is a re-categorisation of children and young people in the youth justice system as 'offenders' rather than children with varied complex needs. Much of the public focus on people who offend and who pose a high risk since 2005 has been concerned with adults, but there are parallels to be drawn with the youth justice system and it is with regard to a category of cases, known as 'serious incidents' in youth justice, that this chapter is concerned.

The Youth Justice Board for England and Wales (YJB) has drawn up a definition of serious incidents that covers both those children and young people who commit certain grave crimes, and captures those children and young people who attempt or commit suicide while under the supervision of a Youth Offending Team (YOT). The accompanying guidance issued by the YJB is to be welcomed for two reasons. Firstly it provides a definition that demonstrates that young people are also victims as well as perpetrators of crime. Secondly, it enables lessons learned from serious incidents to be recorded and analysed, thus providing the potential to influence policy and improve practice in how we deal with young people who offend. However, although the serious incident guidance issued by the YJB has been in place for several years, there is still no official data analysis publicly available. This chapter examines the definition and purpose of the YJB's serious incident guidance, outlines the process itself and considers the likely characteristics of those young people involved in serious incidents in the youth justice system. Recommendations are concluded from the writer's former experience as serious incident manager for the YJB and relevant reports from the joint inspections of YOTs.

Background to YJB serious incident reporting

The YJB is not a national service but has a statutory responsibility to monitor the work of local YOTs and to report findings directly to the home secretary. The YJB guidance on serious incidents was first written in 2001. It was later revised in 2004 to take account of the new YJB regional management structure and to provide more effective linkage with other bodies responsible for the investigation or inquiry into deaths of children in the community or the secure estate for children and young people, in particular the Prison and Probation Ombudsman and new local safeguarding children boards. Further updated guidance has recently been published by YJB (July, 2007).

In short, the definition is as follows: when a serious incident occurs involving a young person supervised by a YOT then a set of procedures apply. YOTs are required to provide an analysis of the serious incident through a local management report (LMR) in the following circumstances:

- the death of a young person in custody in secure accomodation;
- the death or attempted suicide of a young person who is being supervised in the community by a YOT or by another project that the YJB supports, for example ISSP (Intensive Supervision and Surveillance Programme);
- the charge or conviction of a young person either alleged or found to have committed murder, attempted murder, manslaughter or rape while under the statutory supervision of a YOT.

LMRs require an examination of practice where a young person currently being worked with by a YOT commits, or is alleged to have committed, a serious offence as outlined above. This development is consistent with the requirements set by the National Offender Management Service (NOMS) for probation areas. Where the process differs from adult criminal justice services is that emphasis is also placed on the safeguarding of children and young people. LMRs are required when a young person dies in custody, takes his or her own life or attempts to do so while supervised by the YOT, and this provides an insight into cases where young people are also the victims, not only the perpetrators, of a serious incident. This distinction is important as it emphasises the role of YOTs in providing the link between wider children's services and criminal justice agencies. Legislation requires YOTs, through local partnerships, to ensure they protect the needs of children and young people under their supervision while acknowledging that the protection of the public and the management of a young person's risk of future harm are dual tasks. Despite the multi-agency nature of YOTs there remain inherent tensions for staff in balancing the safeguarding of children and the protection of the public. Evidence of this is to be found in a recent annual joint inspection report on YOTs (HMIP, 2006).

The purpose of an LMR is to establish promptly for YOTs if there are any local lessons to be learned from the serious incident and to identify any systemic issues for attention by the YJB. Any action agreed at local level is monitored by YJB regional teams. In exceptional cases following a serious incident notification the YJB may ask HM Inspectorate of Probation (HMIP) to conduct an independent review following the conviction of a young person under YOT supervision. Current public interest in young people and reoffending, particularly while under YOT supervision, may increase the frequency of HMIP input.

While this is helpful in drawing out lessons to be learned in the criminal justice system, there is still work to be undertaken in linking work undertaken by the YJB with other existing statutory frameworks to avoid unnecessary duplication. There have been important changes arising from the 2004 Children Act through the establishment of local safeguarding children boards and it is essential that, where appropriate, liaison occurs between these review bodies and any youth justice serious incident process. There is also a need to look beyond individual cases to consider strategic issues about the safeguarding of children and protection of the public that might warrant a standing commission to oversee child deaths, as recommended by the charity Inquest and its associated literature as 'there are many common concerns that link together individual child deaths, just as there are issues that transcend the narrowly focused remits of specific government departments and state agencies' (Goldson and Coles, 2005: xxiii). At a time of rising custodial rates for children and distorted media messages about the dangers of young people and crime there is even more urgency for accurate analysis of those young people involved in serious incidents.

Unlike probation areas, YOTs do not form part of a national service. They are managed directly by local authority structures through multi-agency management boards comprising representation from police, probation, social services, health and education services. When a young person is involved in a serious incident it may be that local review bodies undertake inquiries into the case, or that the YOT provides a report to its own management board in the first instance. In other cases, local safeguarding children boards may initiate proceedings. As YOTs are accountable directly to local authority structures, the YJB has been unable to require YOTs to comply with all guidance, and ambiguity over accountability has arisen. This may have resulted in some YOTs not reporting a serious incident to the YJB. In restating the reasons behind the production of an LMR it is crucial that the YJB re-emphasises to YOT managers the importance of defensible decision making and management review in what are often complex cases. The LMR is not designed to be a blame exercise but to identify learning points for improved practice and areas for policy development. Given the lack of data available on young people involved in serious incidents in the youth justice system, information held within LMRs may be fundamental to subsequent inquiries or investigations.

Definitions of serious incidents

As established, the YJB serious incident guidance is designed to alert the system to serious incidents where young people harm themselves as well as commit serious further offences. Any snapshot of recent serious incident notifications to the YJB is likely to demonstrate that as many young people attempt suicide, take their lives or are victims of an incident leading to their death as are charged with or receive a conviction for an offence of a serious nature. In understanding more about young people involved in serious incidents, wider currency must be given to this fact, which, although it will not be surprising to many practitioners working directly with young people, is not reflected in the current public perception of young people who offend.

Such evidence is also vital to any discussion on effective approaches to risk management as discussed in other parts of this volume (see Kemshall and Baker, Chapters 1 and 2 in this volume). Practitioners and policy makers should be able to reinforce the fact that the definition of serious incidents in the youth justice system does include the death or attempted suicide of any young person under YOT supervision, and risk management approaches must take into account the issue of vulnerability or risk of harm to self. Furthermore, young women in the youth justice system are even more at risk of harming themselves; serious incidents reported to the YJB are likely to demonstrate that more girls are the victims of suicide attempts or self-harm than are committing serious further offences. A recent study conducted in comprehensive schools in England on the prevalence of deliberate self-harm in adolescents, reported that 'deliberate self-harm was nearly four times more frequent in females than in males' (Hawton and Rodham, 2006). This finding is apparently consistent with research in other countries and information drawn from hospital admissions, and is also likely to reflect YJB data in relation to those YOTs reporting serious incidents. Interestingly, the annual review of YOT inspections for 2005/06, reported that 'girls and young women subject to community orders were significantly more likely to be considered at risk of self harm than boys and youths, and had a greater incidence of both physical and mental health needs' (HMIP, 2006: 41).

Some serious incident cases will also involve young people quite early on in their involvement in the youth justice system, either while on a lower tariff intervention such as a Referral Order or by virtue of their age: 'Serious offending must be distinguished from persistent criminality and many young people who are processed under the grave crimes provisions have had very little previous contact with the criminal justice system' (Nacro, 2002: 20). However, many serious incidents will almost certainly involve 16 and 17 year olds who represent the most significant proportion of the juvenile offending population. Recording the profile of these young people on Asset is fundamental to any risk management approach to ensure that information is fed through to the adult criminal justice system when young people are transferred on to probation supervision at the age of 18 years. Building up a picture of static risk factors and ensuring that offences or behaviour displayed during adolescence are properly taken account of must feature in any developing risk management strategy in youth justice.

Unlike the adult world, offences that involve serious assault (for example, grievous bodily harm, armed robbery, aggravated burglary, affray) are not included in the YJB definition of serious incidents. Instead, the YJB has identified the most serious offences as falling under its serious incidents procedures, and places a priority on improving reporting in relation to these critical few. This prevents too many young people being given the label of having committed a serious incident, although risk management processes must be able to identify entrenched patterns of violence or antisocial behaviour systematically. The recently published YJB serious incident guidance (2007) clarifies the offences included in the definition.

What happens to information about serious incidents in the youth justice system?

Since its revision in 2004, the serious incident guidance procedure has been adapted to provide feedback to YOTs on the learning initiated following completion of the LMR. However, this has not been systematic and the YJB has not yet published a review of lessons learned from serious incidents. This prevents any firm conclusions from being drawn at this stage. A further separate consideration is that as YOTs are directly accountable to local management boards there may be some ambiguity surrounding the status of LMRs and who is responsible for the implementation of recommendations. As part of its national monitoring role undertaken via YJB regional teams, it is essential that the YJB is aware of the necessary action that any local YOT has agreed with its own local management board. This also enables relevant action points to become incorporated into wider performance management systems overseen by the YJB or action plans initiated by YOT inspections.

In the past there has been no mechanism for YOTs to inform the YJB when a case involving a young person results in a conviction in court. As already indicated, some YOTs appeared to be reluctant to complete an LMR when charges were initially brought against a young person. In addition to perceived resource restraints, some YOT practitioners may be reluctant to label a young person with a 'serious crime tag' in case charges are later dropped. Moreover, in the cases where YOTs have completed the documentation to report a serious incident, it is unlikely that the YJB will be informed months later when the outcome of the court case becomes known because there is no formal procedure to do so. Given the serious nature of the offences categorised within the serious incident guidance and the age of some of the young people concerned, this has left both YOTs and the YJB exposed to media publicity and ministerial scrutiny. The YJB is due to issue during 2007 a revised LMR template to include a section regarding notification from the YOT following any subsequent conviction in court. This is intended to rectify the problems outlined above and is part of the newly updated YJB guidance in *Serious incidents* published in the first half of 2007 (Youth Justice Board, 2007).

The YJB is involved in a regular dialogue with HMIP in relation to risk assessment and public protection. This is designed to ensure that HMIP is aware of relevant YJB guidance and that the YJB is kept fully informed of key HMIP findings in this area. It is important that this dialogue continues in order that there is no dissonance between the expectations of the YJB and HMIP in relation to risk assessment and management. There are also opportunities for the YJB to provide HMIP with information relating to serious incidents as part of the pre-inspection process as well as share with HMIP a copy of any analysis of young people involved in serious incidents.

These issues aside, unless the YJB completes its own regular review of serious incidents, it will remain difficult to consolidate the lessons learned from all serious incidents involving young people both as perpetrators and victims. This information must be passed on to YOTs and HMIP as the body responsible for the joint inspection of YOTs and be made available to other relevant inspection or regulatory bodies.

Characteristics of young people involved in serious incidents

For the purpose of this chapter it has not been possible to draw on official data to identify any trends in the age, gender or ethnicity of young people involved in serious incidents in the youth justice system. Experience suggests it is likely that most serious incidents will involve 16 and 17 year olds. It is also probable that girls whose cases fall into the YJB definition of serious incidents are more likely to have attempted to take their own lives or died under YOT supervision. Guidance on the YJB website about serious incidents did not until recently require data on ethnicity so this information will not have been routinely collected.

As would be expected, a range of risk factors are likely to be present among young people involved in serious incidents. These include substance misuse, mental health problems, behavioural difficulties, absence from mainstream education, and accommodation issues. Analysis of which individual factors may have contributed towards a serious incident is complex but should be a necessary feature of every LMR completed and also any review undertaken by the YJB. One barrier to obtaining this information will be in the quality of information provided through

Asset documentation. As HMIP observes in a recent joint inspection annual report (HMIP, 2006), Asset completion is of mixed quality. It is likely that where information is captured it does not clearly attribute risk factors to offending behaviour. It is also unlikely to routinely assess those dynamic factors that contribute to offending. As a result of the constantly changing world in which most adolescents find themselves, the sorts of risk factors they face will change dramatically over short spaces of time and this shifting landscape is not always captured by practitioners and recorded in Asset. Risk assessment is therefore often partial and ineffectual due to changing dynamic factors.

Despite the absence of analysis, it is possible to state fairly confidently that children and young people committing serious incidents will not have received treatment or access to mainstream services. The 2006 annual report from HMIP on YOT inspections supports this claim. It concentrates largely on education and mental health provision and the fact that, while referrals to Children and Adolescent Mental Health Services (CAMHS) have improved, education attendance still remains poor and overall provision is patchy. Recording any outcome in these areas is often overlooked within YOT cases.

It is safe to say that any observation of serious incidents will demonstrate a high number of young people who have been disengaged from mainstream schooling for many years. There is now a body of evidence to show the links between non-participation in education and subsequent delinquency (Stephenson, 2006). Despite the expected statutory links between local education authorities and YOTs, many young people supervised by YOTs do not regularly attend school. Stephenson concludes:

> [b]ecoming detached from ordinary school may, through a series of indirect effects, increase the likelihood of offending, as through the creation of delinquent peer groups both outside school and in segregated education, the increased opportunity for crime, the loss of any positive socialisation of effects of school, the weakening of the levels of supervision, and the increases in the chances of later unemployment through depressed attainment. (Stephenson, 2006: 91)

The first published joint Healthcare Commission and HMIP report on health services and YOTs found that 'children and young people who offend have more health needs than the non-offending population of children. The provision of healthcare for them has improved but it remains inadequate' (Healthcare Commission and HMIP, 2006: 3). This report states that between one sixth and one quarter of YOTs are experiencing problems in gaining access to mental health services. Health outcomes are rarely monitored due to the lack of strategic representation on YOT management boards. HMIP also reports in the annual inspection of YOTs in 2005/6 that 'even where Asset identified a mental health/ substance misuse need associated with offending behaviour a quarter of these children and young people were still not referred on for specialist assessment and/ or treatment' (HMIP, 2006: 41).

These findings therefore, coupled with poor Asset recording as documented in the next section, are evidence that those young people at risk of committing serious further offences, or who are vulnerable of harm to themselves, are likely to have been denied appropriate treatment through CAMHS or education through schooling.

Case management and risk

Asset is the standard assessment tool used by YOTs in all work with young people. Information is obtained about a young person's life and evidence of links between offending behaviour and risk factors recorded under a scoring system. It provides vital documentation for any LMR completed after a serious incident as part of general case management records. However, in a recent annual inspection of YOTs, HMIP found that 'the quality of one in five Assets examined was not sufficient. Worryingly, the proportion considered to be of sufficient quality completed on children and young people convicted of violent offences was significantly lower than those completed on other groups' (HMIP, 2006: 27). Given that Asset is a crucial tool in the management of all young people, but particularly those at risk of serious incidents, it is essential that the use of Asset is reviewed in all serious incident analysis.

Furthermore, any such review of serious incidents in the youth justice system must also consider approaches to risk management as part of all assessment, planning and review of cases. The YJB issued its first guidance on the management of risk in 2005. This guidance (Youth Justice Board, 2005) may therefore not have been disseminated to all YOT practitioners supervising young people until later in that year. However, all YOT managers completing an LMR towards the end of 2005 onwards should have had information and some training made available to them on risk management. Risk-led practice is seen as an important foundation for effective practice with children and young people and is also at the core of public protection. Following an Asset assessment, there should be a subsequent assessment of the likelihood of reoffending and any possible risk of serious harm to others, and, where appropriate, a risk management plan should be developed.

The YJB defines three types of risk outcome: reoffending, serious harm to others and vulnerability (including self-harm). The distinction between these different factors is an important one when considering serious incidents and the links to risk management. Although the three are often associated, it is sometimes the case that a young person can have a high likelihood of reoffending while not necessarily presenting a high risk of serious harm to the public or being considered at risk of self-harm or vulnerable. Other young people might have a low risk of reoffending but the nature of their offences when they do offend can cause victims and the public major distress. In the case of young people in the youth justice system, as this chapter indicates, their behaviour may lead them to commit grave harm to themselves, including the taking of their own lives. How cases involving serious incidents have been managed in relation to the use of a structured risk assessment should be monitored both locally and nationally.

The expectations currently on practitioners are shifting and YOTs will need to ensure that all staff are aware of the requirements of assessment, planning and review in relation to the management of risk. Indeed, the YOT Joint Inspectorate, led by HMIP, now inspects YOTs on this basis and is particularly focused on the need for YOTs to prioritise the risk of harm to others. Although risk factors cannot be removed entirely, the aim should be to mitigate risk. The YJB should consider how to place a risk approach at the centre of YOT practice.

Data provided by HMIP from the first three inspection phases support this. It appears that a 'risk of serious harm' form was routinely completed in 65% of all cases where a positive response was recorded in relation to the relevant indicators in the initial Asset form (HMIP, 2006). However, management oversight of risk of harm cases was only evident in 38% of cases. Some managers did not provide evidence of ever having read a case. In summary, the Joint Inspectorate agreed with the risk of serious harm classification in 78% of cases seen. The annual report on YOT inspections concludes that:

> **work with children and young people considered to pose a risk of harm to others remained an area of ongoing concern. Many YOTs worked with did not complete the full Risk of Harm assessment as required. A full Risk of Harm assessment was not completed on 1 in 4 young people convicted of violent offences. (HMIP, 2006: 27)**

If the emphasis in reviewing any serious incident is on the extent to which a serious further offence or self-harming incident could be prevented, it is fundamental that practitioners are equipped to undertake risk assessments and that managers oversee these decisions. Furthermore, it is crucial that YOTs set up review meetings where young people are categorised as medium or high risk to track progress on individual cases and ensure appropriate case recording of action taken. Where young people also meet multi-agency public protection arrangement (MAPPA) thresholds this is an important tool in managing dynamic risk on a multi-agency basis.

Young people in the youth justice system often lead chaotic and disturbed lives. Combined with undeveloped cognitive behavioural skills, their dynamic risk factors can vary substantially in a short space of time. They can also lack the offending history to build up an accurate picture of static risk so that practitioners fall back on considerable professional discretion in the risk management of young people likely to be involved in serious incidents. YOT staff must be encouraged to support their decisions with a structured risk assessment. Where YOTs submit LMRs following serious incidents, it is vital that any management analysis demonstrates this structured approach to working with the young people who had committed the incidents. This provides evidence of defensible decision making and – in the current media climate with focused public attention on those young people who go on to commit serious further offences – may prevent unfair criticism of how young people are supervised in the community.

Lastly, an absence of structured Asset review and risk management systems may result in young people escalating through the youth justice system into custody. This then places pressure on practitioners to provide other alternatives to community sentencing when young people become persistent and prolific in their offending or antisocial behaviour. Given that some young people involved in serious incidents will be at early stages of offending and only subject to a Referral Order or Final Warning, then risk management is fundamental in trying to address further risk of reoffending or risk of serious harm to others. It can also be a powerful means of minimising the use of custody.

Conclusion

Only a small proportion of the young people known to YOTs across England and Wales will be involved in serious incidents. Most YOTs are unlikely to report more than one or two cases a year to the YJB. Although it is a moot point that the current system of reporting serious incidents does not capture the full extent of the problem, even with more accurate reporting, serious incidents involving young people will undoubtedly still be a small percentage of overall crime committed by young people in England and Wales. There are nearly five and a half million 10 to 17 year olds in England and Wales, and about a quarter of them will have committed an offence in any year (Audit Commission, 2004). Offending by young people represents about a quarter of all recorded crime. Only 3% of young people in England and Wales offend persistently or will be referred to intensive supervision programmes overseen by YOTs (Audit Commission, 2004) and an even smaller percentage of the overall youth crime figures will involve a serious incident. To date, there is no current accurate figure of annual serious incidents as defined by the YJB, as, until very recently, not all serious incidents will have been recorded nationally. The figure may well be less than 200 cases a year. This may come as a surprise to a public whose views of young people and crime are driven by media stories of antisocial behaviour and violence.

It is therefore imperative that further analysis is undertaken on the group of young people involved in serious incidents, as defined by the YJB, to ensure that:

- serious incidents involving young people are properly considered as part of wider measures to safeguard children;

- any public protection measures to manage those who offend and pose a high risk take account of the particular characteristics of children and young people involved in serious incidents.

Given current political, media and public scrutiny into criminal justice services, there are benefits for the YJB in being able to present a national overview of the types of serious incidents involving young people to help prevent them occurring. Furthermore, as so many young people are equally at risk of self-harm or are vulnerable to a range of problems, the YJB definition of 'serious incidents' is more wide reaching than in the adult criminal justice world. This is entirely appropriate.

The LMRs from YOTs submitted to the YJB following a serious incident outline the difficult job many practitioners face in working with young people. Many of the young people concerned lead chaotic and often troubled lives and it is extremely hard to manage their multiple needs. It is always easier with the benefit of hindsight to observe how a case might have been more effectively managed. However, there are areas of supervision, management and review for which YOTs must ensure they have necessary procedures in place supported by evidence of defensible decision making.

National oversight and a regular review of serious incidents taking place in the youth justice system may help bring into perspective the problems YOT practitioners face in working with young people in the youth justice system. At a time of crisis, with prison numbers escalating and ministers under pressure to be tough on youth crime, such evidence should provide better understanding of the children and young people involved in serious incidents and how best to manage the risks they present.

References

Audit Commission (2004) *Youth justice 2004*, London: Audit Commission.

Goldson, B. and Coles, D. (2005) *In the care of the state? Child deaths in penal custody in England and Wales*, London: Inquest.

Hawton, K. and Rodham, K. (2006) *By their own hand: Deliberate self-harm and suicidal ideas in adolescents*, London: Jessica Kingsley.

Healthcare Commission and HMI Probation (2006) *Let's talk about it: A review of healthcare in the community for young people who offend*, London: Home Office.

HM Inspectorate of Probation (2006) *Joint inspection of YOTs 2005/6*, London: Home Office.

Home Office (2006) *Young people and crime: Findings from the 2005 Offending, Crime And Justice Survey*, London: Home Office.

Hough, M. and Roberts, J. (2004) *Youth crime and youth justice*, Bristol: The Policy Press.

Nacro (2002) *Children who commit grave crimes*, London: Nacro.

Stephenson, M. (2006) *Young people and offending: Education, youth justice and social inclusion*, London: Willan.

Youth Justice Board (2005) *Managing risk in the community*, London: Youth Justice Board.

Youth Justice Board (2007) *Serious Incidents: Guidence on serious incident reporting procedures*, London: Youth Justice Board.

Working with young people in a culture of public protection

6

Mike Nash

Introduction

This chapter has two aims. One is to establish if there is such a thing as a culture of public protection and the other is to determine if this will impact upon the working practices of those involved in Youth Offending Teams (YOTs). A brief review of recent penal trends will set the context for the growth in public protection processes and cultures. This will then suggest ways in which criminal justice agencies, and key decisions, are affected by an increasingly risk-averse agenda. If it is accepted that public protection policies have brought about changes in criminal justice cultures then consideration needs to be given to their possible impact upon a discrete and well-established culture that aims to put the needs and welfare of young people first.

The background to a cultural transformation?

It is unlikely that many would argue with the view that penal policy has become increasingly punitive since the election of the Labour government in 1997. This punitiveness has taken on several guises but is typified as follows: longer sentencing, mandatory sentences, the use of civil measures to restrain and contain those who offend in the community, the criminalisation of antisocial behaviour, restricted release arrangements and a focus on compliance and enforcement (see for example Dunbar and Langdon, 1998; James and Raine, 1998; Matthews and Young, 2003; Tonry, 2004; Hughes, 2007). One aspect above all has perhaps driven this agenda and that is protecting the public from potentially dangerous people who offend. The initial thrust of this agenda was focused upon sex offenders with the creation of the sex offender register in the 1997 Sex Offenders Act. Because immediate loopholes were spotted in the legislation (those whose sentences ended before the register was created, and were therefore not eligible for registration), civil restraints were invoked under the 1998 Crime and Disorder Act in the form of sex offender orders. In essence, these orders introduced the idea of, in effect, punishing people for something they *might* do in the future. If a person had a previous history of sexual offending and was placing himself in a position of potential harm to others, he could be prevented from doing any number of things to reduce the *potential* risk. Elsewhere, this focus upon risk prevention or management had been backed up by the formal establishment of multi-agency public protection arrangements (MAPPA) in the 2000 Criminal Justice Court Services Act. The scene was set therefore for a huge expansion of the risk industry (see Kemshall, Chapter 1 in this volume) with predatory paedophiles in the government's firing line. With such a popular target there was little public opposition and it became a difficult agenda for agencies to resist. Alternative ideas or ways of working were regarded as 'soft' and on the side of the person who had offended, by definition playing down the importance of victims' rights. It is this last point that is perhaps of most relevance to the present discussion. The question is, has public protection work developed its own culture, and, if so, what is its impact upon traditional working practices (and cultures) of the agencies involved?

Changing cultures in a punitive world

Much has already been written about the potential effect of closer collaboration between agencies working to a public protection agenda. Nash (1999) introduced the idea of a 'polibation officer', in essence a fusion of police and probation roles. At this time there was a suspicion that probation 'culture', typified by a humanitarian approach to those who offend (Vanstone, 2004), would be swamped by police values (crime control), especially as the common agenda was focused upon potentially dangerous and very unpopular people who offend. The climate was therefore likely to be unforgiving and less tolerant of therapeutic interventions. Kemshall and Maguire (2001) discussed the 'policification' of probation work and Mawby and Worrall (2004) extended the notion into a discussion on prolific offender projects. More recently, Mawby et al (2007) have questioned the move towards 'prisi-polibation' with the creation of the National Offender Management Service (NOMS) and the concept of end-to-end offender management. Thus there appears to be a view that multi-agency working, especially on specific projects, may have an impact upon individual or traditional agency practice and culture. The extent of this impact may be debated but there would appear to be a consensus that there is undoubtedly an effect. If the object of collaboration is public protection, with its undoubtedly high profile, then it is possible that the impact will be greater as agencies aim for consistency of approach and message. It is this high-profile external world in which public protection is conducted that probably has most impact upon the agencies involved and may lead to the emergence of a specific culture.

Public protection work is therefore shaped by its external environment. It is undoubtedly the case that the traditional supervision of high-risk, potentially dangerous offenders was quietly (and quite secretly) carried out by probation officers and mental health staff. There is little evidence that this system was ineffective and, indeed, some say it worked well (Coker and Martin, 1985). However, a number of serious offences committed by those under some form of supervision have given this aspect of practice a very high public profile. In particular, a number of public inquiries into homicides and serious child abuse have pointed to failures of communication as a main cause of tragedy. Partly as a result, MAPPA now seek to ensure that individual agencies work together to assess, manage and aim to reduce risk. Implicit in this process is a view that communication between agencies should be better, quicker and more effective (although this perhaps overlooks the idea that it is not communication per se that is answer, but what is done with the information once it is received). However, the real problem for the public protection process is twofold. The first is that it is defined by failure rather than success. No one gets to hear of the number of high-risk cases who do not reoffend but everyone hears about those who do. Secondly, each of these failures leads to the government taking measures to strengthen the process further (as well as changes to existing legislation or new legislation), with subsequent failures seeing this process repeated in cyclical fashion. Perfect public protection is an impossible goal and failure is inevitable. Unfortunately, this appears only in subtexts within government announcements, which prefer to focus instead on statements such as 'public protection better than ever' (Home Office, 2004).

In this wider context, therefore, a number of features of public protection begin to emerge. Perhaps the most dominant of these might be described as 'risk aversion', where agencies become much more reluctant to take 'risks' with offender decisions and so 'play safe'. Certainly, over the past few years, the pressure generated by cases going wrong has been enormous. Cases of serious further offending by those under supervision in the community on parole licence have pointed the finger of blame at a number of agencies and aspects of their practice. Two reviews of serious further offence cases by HM Chief Inspector of Probation (HMIP, 2006a and 2006b) gained widespread publicity and identified traditional failings in communication and risk assessment, among other problems. A number of other cases pointed to a failure of the parole system with clear implications that the Parole Board had got it wrong in authorising release for those who offended again in serious fashion. Headlines such as, 'Prisoners freed under supervision carried out 61 violent crimes' (Cowan, 2006) fuel public concern, although perhaps more should be made of the percentages committed by those with only low- and medium-risk ratings (Bridges, 2006). The upshot of these high-profile tragedies is a new assault on so-called 'soft' legislation and practice. The then home secretary, John Reid, proposed changes to the automatic prisoner release system, to the way in which tariffs in life and public protection sentences are calculated, and insisted on Parole Board members having a victim perspective in their deliberations. The whole thrust of recent policy announcement has been a move away from offender rights towards those of victims. This philosophy is encapsulated in Reid's proposals to 're-balance the criminal justice system in favour of the victim and the law-abiding majority' (Home Office, 2006: 4).

Criminal justice practitioners are therefore now operating in a climate where failure, although sadly occasionally inevitable, will be met with a frenzy of media blame and, one suspects, little support from government ministers. A reluctance to take any form of risk is therefore likely. For example, a BBC report (Monday 6 November 2006, http://news.bbc.co.uk/1/hi/uk/6119576.stm) noted a drop in the number of lifers released on parole, suggesting that since April 2006 the Parole Board had granted release in only one in nine cases (approximately 50% down on the previous year). The chairman of the Board, Sir Duncan Nichol, admitted that they were being more cautious after the high-risk cases reported on by HM Inspectorate of Probation (2006a and 2006b). He suggested that so-called model prisoners would receive greater scrutiny and that in future the Board '... will be absolutely sure before release' (BBC news report, as noted above). Unfortunately, well-intentioned comments such as this only serve to feed the anger and condemnation the next time a case goes wrong. The only way to be absolutely sure would be to stop early release completely. In passing, it is worth recalling another BBC news report from 11 May 2000, suggesting that the Parole Board had been too cautious in *not releasing* enough prisoners to reduce the size of the prison population.

Working with young people who offend

How does this climate of risk reduction, risk aversion and quest for certainty affect those who work with young offenders? Multi-agency working is at the heart of working with young people who offend, just as it is with public protection. YOTs were established by sections 37–42 of the 1998 Crime and Disorder Act with the specific intention to 'prevent offending by young people aged 10–17', but, more than this, the White Paper introducing the Act made a bold statement challenging the heart of work with young people. In 'No More Excuses' it was argued that, '[c]oncerns about the welfare of young people have too often been seen as in conflict with the aims of protecting the public' (Home Office, 1997: s2.1). However, as Leng et al (1998: 68) argue, there was not a specific requirement of crime prevention for all agencies involved in YOTs, so social workers, for example, could continue with a paramount interest in the young person's welfare. If, however, we accept that traditional cultures, such as that of probation officers to 'advise, assist and befriend', have been challenged almost to non-existence, what might be the impact on a specific way of working with young people? YOTs are members of MAPPA and as such are exposed to cultures of public protection that are essentially determined by a response to certain types of adults who offend. Although within their own multi-agency frameworks the welfare of the child may remain paramount, to what extent will this be compromised in a public protection setting? Within the MAPPA, YOTs are but one professional grouping among many whose ethos has been shifted by a number of external events, pressures and changes to legislation. It is undoubtedly a significant challenge to maintain their professional focus within this environment.

For a long period, the debate has focused around an either/or dichotomy of punishment and welfare. However, Muncie suggests that this is inadequate:

> What is clear is that traditional justice vs. welfare or welfare vs. punishment
> debates are particularly inadequate in unravelling how youth justice acts on an

> amalgam of rationales, oscillating around, but also beyond, the caring ethos of social services, the neo-liberal legalistic ethos of responsibility and the neo-conservative ethos of punishment and coercion. (Muncie, 2006: 771)

Muncie continues by suggesting that what might once have been regarded as indicators of the need for welfare support are now read as possible precursors for criminality (2006: 781), in other words, need is conceptualised as risk. Thus ever-earlier intervention is justified as a pre-emptive strike and, as a consequence, failure to 'take advantage' may result in stiffer penalties later on (Blair, 1997, quoted in Muncie, 2006: 782).

Therefore, as a result of the wider conception of youth and young people as posing risks to the existing order and becoming the criminalised 'other', the long-established welfare rhetoric becomes transformed into risk, and relatively common social problems become redefined as criminogenic risk factors. Thus it might be argued that the case to put children first (which means regarding them as children to begin with), is already under threat, before issues of public protection enter the fray. Lovell and Evans ask, '[w]here is the public outrage and high profile political agenda to tackle the low reporting and conviction rates for violence and abuse of children, in many cases the very same children who are ending up in our jails?' (2007: 8). Writers on the subject in the UK and elsewhere have argued that young people are increasingly mistrusted and problematised (see for example Kelly, 2000, 2003; Stephen and Squires, 2004). However, the issue is whether or not these attitudes are reflected in the ways in which young people are handled within the criminal justice and youth offending (no longer youth justice, of course) systems and, indeed, whether or not the focus on their youth status is likely to be lost. Muncie (2006: 784) reminds us that the number of 15 to 17 year olds in prison establishments increased from 769 in 1993 to 2,089 in 2002. He adds that in 1992 approximately 100 children under 15 were sentenced to custody, rising to 800 in 2001 (an increase of 800%). According to figures released by the Youth Justice Board (YJB), in November 2006 the under-18 custodial population stood at 2,995, with a further 3,281 18–19 year olds incarcerated. Finally, Muncie notes the increase in antisocial behaviour orders (ASBOs) for 10–17 year olds, from 84 in 2001 to 509 in 2003. With approximately 30% breached and half of these receiving custody (Muncie, 2006: 783), the problematising of young people's behaviour is clearly resulting in a much-expanded criminalised and incarcerated group.

Perhaps the bottom line of the debate concerning young people and crime is whether or not they should be treated differently from adults, either because they are chronologically younger or because they are emotionally less mature. If the latter position is supported it would require a suspension of the increasing demonisation of youth, a position that the media and politicians appear, at present, unwilling to embrace. A study of public attitudes concerning the punishment of young people who offend in Canada (Varma, 2006) offers some clues in this respect. One of Varma's general points, in summarising earlier research in the field, is that the public do not see differences in the seriousness of offences based upon the age of the person who has offended. In other words, a serious crime is a serious crime no matter the age of the culprit. Support for this general notion would come from the media treatment of, and public response to, the murder of 2-year-old James Bulger by Robert Thompson and Jon Venables, both aged 10 at the time. Headlines from newspapers such as the *Daily Mail* (25 November 1993), 'Evil, brutal and cunning' (Thompson, 1998: 96) clearly ascribe adult propensities to children, the seriousness of the crime overriding age and developmental issues. The *Sunday Telegraph* (21 February 1993) encapsulated the thoughts of many regarding young people when they described the murder as the 'double death of innocence' (Thompson, 1998: 128). The virtual doubling of the original eight-year tariff by home secretary Michael Howard is also indicative of a media-driven penal policy (a 20,000-signature petition had been sent in by a major tabloid newspaper). Indeed, because the perpetrators were children themselves, this appeared to exacerbate the perceived seriousness of the crime (contrast this with the response to a similar crime committed in Norway at about the same time, Muncie, 2005: 53).

So what does this mean for the greater involvement of victims and their relatives in the sentencing and release process? Will these people be able to step beyond grief and anger and regard perpetrators as vulnerable young people, or will punishment be a dominant feeling? Is the media/public response to the Bulger murderers typical of what we might expect when young people commit very serious crimes and will this feed into the 'official' process? If public (and agency?) perceptions of crime seriousness are not apparently lessened by the age of the perpetrator (Varma, 2006: 177), what about their attitudes to punishment? Varma suggests that, in reviewing a number of studies, the age of the person has less impact upon attitudes towards punishment than does the provision of a greater amount of information concerning the person. In other words, the more the public know about a person who has offended the less punitive they become. However, a good deal was known about Venables and Thompson and this appeared to have had little impact upon attitudes towards their punishment, other than making it more severe. As Varma notes, there appears to be social agreement about the seriousness of crime, irrespective of the age of the person who has offended, and this may override other considerations (2006: 177). It appears as if information about the young person may alter perceptions but these are only likely to be influential if they portray the young person as a victim also, or at least to have suffered sufficiently to engender public sympathy.

Thus, there appears to be an enduring tension in society regarding our perceptions of and attitudes towards children and young people who commit very serious crimes. If we accept that the perceived seriousness of a criminal act will be the main (public) factor, then we need to consider how much this might impact upon a consideration of age and development issues in sentencing and release decisions. The culture of public protection, certainly in the adult domain, appears to be fuelled more by repeated incidents than by one-off occurrences. This was less the case with the Bulger murder as this was regarded as a one-off that signalled the emergence of a wider moral and social malaise, and was all the worse *because* it was committed by young children. The issue for those working with children and young adults who offend is the extent to which they can step outside the hype surrounding *offences* to maintain a focus on the *offender*. As we have already noted, it is now much more common to talk of risks rather than dangerousness. However, it should be of concern that assessments of risk might utilise factors that, to a certain extent, have been based upon perceptions of 'problem' behaviour. These problems, construed as criminogenic, may equally be representative of the type of needs that young people in a range of social settings have, and are dealt with, without the individual becoming labelled as a 'risk'.

A key element here will be how multi-agency public protection panels (MAPPPs) respond to children and young people who seriously offend. Will these panels, increasingly marked by a risk-averse practice, take the 'risk' of allowing for the youthfulness of some of the young people under consideration? A public protection culture might be typified by both defensible and defensive decision making, by erring on the side of caution and perhaps by 'going along with' some of the more spectacular constructions of dangerousness that have more to do with notoriety than routine, everyday serious offending. Accommodating the needs of a young person into this situation may be difficult. Of course, one way of going towards ensuring that this does happen is for the component agencies of MAPPPs to retain a distinctive culture or ethos of their own. However, the very nature of MAPPPs, especially in the adult field to date, has seen a tendency towards a more uniform view determined by the language of risk (Kemshall and Maguire, 2001).

Effective assessment of risk is dependent not only upon gathering as much information as possible, but also on making the *best* use of it. It also requires a constant updating of the information and analysis, especially in the case of young people who may be changing and developing at a rapid rate. Sheldrick (1999: 506) commented on the strength of having a number of different agencies involved in assessment and decision making for young people, but stresses that this strength comes from a *variety* of perspectives, rather than a homogeneous one. She believes that any one professional needs to stick strictly to the limit of their skills. She goes on to say that professionals need to use their skills to gain as much detailed information as possible and that small, seemingly obscure pieces of information may be vital. Of course, the unstated point here is that the practitioner needs to be skilled at interviewing children and young people; there may, in other words, be a need for specific techniques and indeed a specific attitude towards the needs and circumstances of a particular group of young people.

Conclusion

It is extremely difficult to say that an organisation has one type of culture or another. Not only is it problematic to put boundaries around such a complex idea, but it is also very likely that any organisation will have a number of cultures. They will be subject to a variety of influences over time, from within and without. Changes may evolve naturally or be forced by external policy. Cultures are also likely to have arisen in specific contexts and have been located within one organisation. The rapid growth of multi-agency working has challenged that notion.

This chapter has explored whether or not a specific type of culture, based upon public protection, has begun to emerge and whether it is having a significant impact upon the work of NOMS and YOTs, indeed if it has supplanted existing cultures within those organisations. For NOMS it is probably fair to say that there has been a long-standing challenge to what might be termed probation's traditional culture. Features of this challenge would be higher levels of management, greater audit, an evidence-based approach, national standards and accredited programmes. In other words, the traditional ways of working – which were the practical face of that culture – were deemed to be ineffective and outdated. Thus new probation recruits have, over the past 15 years or so, joined an organisation whose culture has already been modified and whose new entrants have effectively signed up to the new mandate. The emergence of public protection has effectively cemented that cultural change more deeply within the organisation. This culture encompasses an attitude to certain young people that is difficult to challenge. Protecting the vulnerable presses all the right buttons for the media and therefore politicians jump on board with enthusiasm. For organisations such as the probation service it is not so much if they will do this work, but more a case of how much, what controls they have over it, and the ways in which it might affect other areas of practice. It has been argued here that this public protection culture is hugely influential and is undoubtedly becoming a defining ethos for the probation service. Furthermore, the way in which public protection policy and practice is configured makes it increasingly easy to push other, traditional areas of probation practice down the agenda. Indeed, it is likely that a number of these 'social' aspects of the job will be passed to other organisations. For the probation service, then, the question might be if a new type of organisation forms itself around the new culture, will a discrete public protection agency emerge (public protection teams already in existence)? Or, if not, will the probation service increasingly only work with people who offend who pose a high risk (in a particular way) and by default leave behind many of its former activities?

If this transformation of probation culture is under way and becoming embedded, where do other services who work with young people sit? Perhaps for youth offending services there is a shorter history of the type of cultural challenge and transformation experienced by the probation service. Nonetheless, change is undoubtedly under way and a number of centralising tendencies are evident. Offending youth have also, as noted earlier, become politicised as dangerous offenders and, as such, subjected to increasingly punitive measures. This in itself is enough for continuing debate, but the inclusion of public protection issues in working with young people who offend poses other questions. When it comes to dealing with very serious offending, the enduring issue about children and young people's rights is exaggerated. The home secretary, John Reid, made his views clear in the proposals to rebalance the rights distribution within the criminal justice system (Home Office, 2006). If young people who offend in general are now viewed as having too many rights at the expense of victims, then what of the special rights of young people?

For those who champion the cause of young people's welfare, there may be some hope in the structures of services for young people who offend. There are 157 YOTs set up by an extremely diverse range of local authorities. The actual component elements of YOTs are therefore likely to vary far more than the MAPPAs (of which there are 42) and the latter may be more susceptible to the national agenda. As argued above, however, it may be more difficult to maintain the welfare focus within MAPPAs (when in a minority) than in the YOTs themselves.

If MAPPAs do foster a distinctive culture, then what of the special focus on young people? Can a culture that aims to put children and young people first and supports a distinct approach to their offending within the criminal justice process survive? Much of course will depend upon the political and media context and whether or not other 'demons' are found for them to focus upon. However, for the foreseeable future, public protection from people who offend and pose a high risk is going to govern many aspects of criminal justice practice. The agenda is difficult to resist and its impact has already been considerable in the work of the probation service, with adults and young people who offend. It could possibly lead to the formation of a new type of organisation, or at least very discrete operational practice. For those working exclusively with young people, the challenge may well be retaining a multi-agency culture that is focused upon the needs of young people at least as much as it is in managing the risks they pose. They should look to the example of the 'losses' experienced by the probation service and really think about the potential loss of a very important culture.

References

Bridges, A. (2006) 'Working with dangerous offenders: What is achievable?' unpublished paper, London: School of Oriental and African Studies, University of London, 15 November 2006.

Coker, J.B. and Martin, J.P. (1985) *Licensed to live*, Oxford: Basil Blackwell.

Cowan, R. 'Prisoners freed under supervision carried out 61 violent crimes', *The Guardian*, 24 October 2006.

Dunbar, I. and Langdon, A. (1998) *Tough justice: Sentencing and penal policies in the 1990s*, London: Blackstone Press.

HM Inspectorate of Probation (2006a) *An independent review of a serious further offence case: Anthony Rice*, London: Home Office.

HM Inspectorate of Probation (2006b) *An independent review of a serious further offence case: Damien Hanson & Elliot White*, London: Home Office.

Home Office (1997) *No more excuses: A new approach to tackling youth crime in England and Wales*, Cm 3809, London: The Stationery Office.

Home Office (2004) press release for 2004 MAPPA report (available at: www. probation.homeoffice.gov.uk/output/Page241.asp, accessed 17 January 2007).

Home Office (2006) *Rebalancing the criminal justice system in favour of the law-abiding majority: Cutting crime, reducing reoffending and protecting the public*, London: Home Office.

Hughes, G. (2007) *The politics of crime and community*, Basingstoke: Macmillan.

James, A. and Raine, J. (1998) *The new politics of criminal justice*, Harlow: Longman.

Kelly, P. (2000) 'The dangerousness of youth-at-risk: the possibilities of surveillance and intervention in uncertain times', *Journal of Adolescence*, vol 23, no 4, pp 463–76.

Kelly, P. (2003) 'Growing up as risky business? Risks, surveillance and the institutionalised mistrust of youth', *Journal of Youth Studies*, vol 6, no 2, pp 165–80.

Kemshall, H. and Maguire, M. (2001) 'Public protection, partnership and risk penality: The multi-agency risk management of sexual and violent offenders', *Punishment & Society*, vol 3, no 2, pp 237–64.

Leng, R., Taylor, R. and Wasik, M. (1998) *Blackstone's guide to the Crime and Disorder Act 1999*, London: Blackstone Press.

Lovell, L. and Evans, K. (2007) 'Tough on youth crime and tough on young people', *Criminal Justice Matters*, no 66, winter, pp 8–10.

Matthews, R. and Young, J. (2003) *The new politics of crime and punishment*, Cullompton: Willan.

Mawby, R.C., Crawley, P. and Wright, A. (2007) 'Beyond "polibation" and towards "prisi-polibation"? Joint agency offender management in the context of the Street Crime Initiative', *International Journal of Police Science and Management*, vol 9, no 2, pp 122-34.

Mawby, R. and Worrall, A. (2004) '"Polibation" revisited: Policing, probation and prolific offender projects', *International Journal of Police Science and Management*, vol 6, no 2, pp 63–73.

Muncie, J. (2005) 'The globalization of crime control – The case of youth and juvenile justice: Neo-liberalism, policy convergence and international convention', *Theoretical Criminology*, vol 9, no 10, pp 35–62.

Muncie, J. (2006) 'Governing young people: Coherence and contradiction in contemporary youth justice', *Critical Social Policy*, vol 26, no 4, pp 770–93.

Nash, M. (1999) 'Enter the "polibation officer"', *International Journal of Police Science and Management*, vol 11, nos 4 and 5, pp 252–61.

Sheldrick, S. (1999) 'Practitioner review: The assessment and management of risk in adolescents', *Journal of Child Psychology and Psychiatry*, vol 40, no 4, pp 507–18.

Stephen, D.E. and Squires, P. (2004) 'They're still children and entitled to be children: Problematising the institutionalised mistrust of marginalised youth in Britain', *Journal of Youth Studies*, vol 7, no 3, pp 352–69.

Thompson, K. (1998) *Moral panics*, London: Routledge.

Tonry, M. (2004) *Punishment and politics: Evidence and emulation in the making of English crime control policy*, Cullompton: Willan.

Vanstone, M. (2004) 'Mission control: The origins of a humanitarian service', *Probation Journal*, vol 31, no 1, pp 34–47.

Varma, K.N. (2006) 'Face-ing the offender: Examining public attitudes towards young offenders', *Contemporary Justice Review*, vol 9, no 2, pp 175–87.

Never too early? Reflections on research and interventions for early developmental prevention of serious harm

7

Ros Burnett

Introduction

When in autumn 2006 the government introduced plans for intervening at the perinatal stage and in the babyhood of children growing up in dysfunctional families (Cabinet Office, 2006), media discussions raised the spectres of foetal antisocial behaviour orders ('fasbos'), and electronic monitoring companies forcing their way into the homes of large families and unmarried teenage mothers in order to 'tag' their toddlers. The influence of research on recent strategies for 'stopping it before it starts' is plain to see. At a Downing Street seminar on social exclusion, Blair (2006) pointed out: 'There is now a wealth of empirical data to analyse. The purport of it is clear. You can detect and predict the children and families likely to go wrong'. In the context of issues debated in the present volume, and the recent 'shift from a post- to a pre-crime society … in which the possibility of forestalling risks competes with and even takes precedence over responding to wrongs done' (Zedner, 2007: 262), our misgivings in reaction to these developments in policy should be clear (see especially Boswell and Nash, Chapters 3 and 6 in this volume). Viewed pessimistically, the prospect of a society in which individuals are locked up for crimes that they have not committed, purely on the basis of prediction, as depicted in the film Minority Report (2002) seems to draw ever nearer. Yet, realistic concern about the possible drift of such strategies should not blind us to the existence and value of a substantial body of research into early risk factors associated with subsequent antisocial behaviour and early preventive interventions.

This research on early developmental risk factors and interventions is useful, not least because it helps in differentiating low-risk, 'normal' behaviours from the high-risk, more serious forms of the behaviours and vulnerability that concern us in this volume. Criminal career and longitudinal studies commonly identify different types of groups of young people who offend and pathways (trajectories) into and out of crime, each with distinguishing characteristics that can be traced back to infancy. Moffitt (1993) has famously contrasted 'adolescent limited' with 'life-course persistent' offending. This theoretical distinction accords with common knowledge of many young people who go through a phase of lawbreaking in adolescence but quickly grow out of it, in contrast to a minority who have a history of conduct problems from early childhood and who seem more deeply involved in a criminal lifestyle. There is continuing debate about whether such typologies are helpful, or empirically supported, but all longitudinal studies identify a small group within the larger cohort who receive significantly more convictions (generally including violence), who are more victimised and have more sociopsychological problems and who generally start such behaviour sooner and persist longer. Research on early years contributes to understanding the initial set of circumstances that, left alone, cumulate into more deep-rooted and complex problems. This chapter points, selectively, to findings from this research base and then considers some of the practical and ethical problems, which it raises. I conclude that the concept of early intervention should not be dismissed outright and that most important is the way programmes are developed, and their objectives and outcomes.

A brief look at the research base

There is a voluminous literature on the antecedents of crime and antisocial behaviour, some of it overlapping with, and some of it separate from, research on the precursors of psychopathology (mental disorders), though the starting point for much of this is after children have reached school age. This research has led to the 'risk-factor prevention paradigm', in which 'the basic idea [is to] identify the key risk factors for offending and implement prevention methods designed to counteract them. There is often a related attempt to identify key protective factors against offending' (Farrington, 2000: 1–2). The focus in the present chapter is on aspects of this literature that are pertinent to the development of more serious harm (violent crime, severe and chronic antisocial behaviour), and on pre-school-age children. In the space available it is only possible to have a whistle-stop tour of selected prominent or relevant studies and reviews.[1]

The 'risk-factor prevention paradigm' is founded on several prospective longitudinal studies that have followed up cohorts of individuals since early childhood. Notable among these are: the Cambridge Study of Delinquent Development (led by David Farrington) and the Pittsburgh Youth Study (led by Rolf Loeber). The latter was coordinated with the Denver Youth Survey and the Rochester Youth Development Study. Each of these commenced when the children were already of school age. Of separate provenance, and studying children from birth, another renowned longitudinal study is the Dunedin Multidisciplinary Health and Development

---

[1] See Farrington and Welsh (2006) for a recent review of research findings on early risk factors for offending, protective factors and early prevention programmes. Note that much of this research is focused on males, though some of the longitudinal studies include females.

Study, based in New Zealand (with which Terrie Moffitt and Absolom Caspi are associated). There has increasingly been collaboration between separate teams in order to develop theory and integrate findings.

The Cambridge Study in Delinquent Development, a prospective longitudinal survey of 400 London males beginning at age 8, found that the best predictors at age 8 to 10 for the core 5%–6% who received around half of all criminal convictions obtained by this sample are: 'troublesomeness' (as rated by peers and teachers), daring or risk taking (rated by peers and parents), family members with criminal convictions, low family income, low school attainment and poor concentration in class (Farrington, 2005). Other childhood variables that are associated with the risk of offending chronically are hyperactivity-impulsivity attention problems, conduct disorder and callous-unemotional behaviour that is similar to adult psychopathy (Coid, 2003). The interaction between neighbourhood effects, lifestyle and individual characteristics has been neglected in research (Sampson et al, 2002). A more recent, cross-sectional study has shown community variables (especially neighbourhood and school) to be highly correlated with involvement in crime during adolescence (Wikström and Butterworth, 2006).

There are fewer studies that commenced with birth cohorts or children of pre-school age, but a recent review (Shaw and Gross, 2006: 27–8) identified associations (sometimes modest) between the following early childhood attributes and later serious antisocial behaviour:

- characteristics of the prenatal environment (for example, tobacco and alcohol use, maternal age, perinatal complications);
- social adversity during early childhood (for example, poverty, quality of parenting, cumulative family adversity);
- child disruptive behaviour emerging around age 2 (modest association) and at age 3 (stronger association) though only a subgroup go on to demonstrate early-starting severe antisocial behaviour (linked with compromised parenting and family adversity);
- hostile, rejecting and abusive parenting during the infant's early childhood.

Although multiple risk factors have *interactive* effects, Shaw and Gross tentatively point to some risk factors that have an *independent* and cumulative impact on the development of delinquent behaviour, including child maltreatment and harsh parenting.

Another review of longitudinal studies (Haapasalo and Pokela, 1998) focused specifically on the relationship between negative child-rearing practices (child abuse and child neglect) and later criminality to explore evidence for the hypothesis that violence breeds violence. The analysis found that, among other variables, corporal punishment, authoritarian and power-assertive parental discipline, rejection, abuse, as well as lax parenting, were predictors of aggressive, criminal and antisocial behaviour.

Findings from the Dunedin Study overlap with risk-factor studies but this research team has focused more on the biological basis of antisocial behaviour as well as environmental factors, and on formulating an understanding of causal mechanisms in the development of antisocial behaviour. This study, carried out over the last 30 years, is one of the largest longitudinal investigations of human development. A cohort of 1,037 New Zealand children (52% male), born in 1972–73, have been followed since the age of 3 to track their health, behaviour and circumstances. In the initial study, the authors used rater impressions of children's behaviours during 90 minutes of psychological tests with the aim of examining associations with later reports and official criminal records of antisocial behaviour during middle childhood, adolescence and adulthood.

From this research, neuropsychological factors and maltreatment (abuse) have emerged as critical in explaining the long-term continuity of conduct disorders and extreme antisocial behaviour. Studies have shown infant neural development to be influenced by poor prenatal nutrition, prenatal exposure to toxic agents, physical abuse early in life, as well as heritable individual differences in neuropsychological health. Moffitt identifies two kinds of neuropsychological 'deficits': verbal and 'executive' (including inattention and impulsivity) and proposes that the antecedents are present before or soon after birth:

> It is possible that the etiological chain begins with some factor capable of producing individual differences in the neuropsychological functions of the infant nervous system. Factors that influence infant neural development are myriad, and many of them have been empirically linked to antisocial outcomes. (Moffitt, 1993: 680)

In stressing the association between dysfunctions of the nervous system and persistent conduct disorders, Moffitt (1993: 685) asserts that 'biological origins are in no way deterministic. Rather, individual variations in nervous system health provide raw material for subsequent person–environment interactions'.

Another strand of this research programme is investigating environmental–genetic interactions. After biogenetic research had identified a link between monoamine oxidase A (MAOA) and propensities to violence (in mice and humans), Caspi et al (2002) obtained DNA from a subsample of boys in the Dunedin cohort to carry out a study of the interactions between extreme parenting and MAOA activity. By the time of study the participants were 26 years of age. Maltreatment in infancy or harsh physical discipline were found to have a direct effect on rates of adolescent conduct disorder, antisocial personality disorder and convictions for violent offences. However, these associations were considerably greater for individuals in whom the expression of MAOA activity was low.

Very early preventive interventions

The policy implications of this research on early risk factors, Farrington (2000) argues, can be likened to medical research that identifies the precursors of a disease, thereby indicating which circumstances and behaviours should be avoided. Similarly, preventive measures are indicated to reduce the likelihood of involvement in crime, with the possibility of eliminating other social problems that are associated with crime, such as substance abuse and chronic unemployment (Farrington, 2000). Because of the early onset of persistent antisocial conduct, the benefit of earlier prevention strategies is indicated. 'Developmental approaches', as the name suggests, are those designed to tackle factors associated with later antisocial behaviour and disadvantage, and may be 'primary' (aimed at the community as a whole) or 'secondary' (targeting those categorised as at risk), in contrast to 'tertiary' prevention, targeting those who have already been convicted and therefore occurring much later.

The results of very early (pre-school) interventions are promising. A meta-analytical review concluded that 'there are enduring cognitive, social-emotional, and parent-family impacts of preschool programs, all of which are similar in magnitude. The "head start" that children receive does make a difference in the long run' (Nelson et al, 2003: 27). Probably the best known of such programmes are the US-based High/Scope Perry Preschool Project and the Olds's Prenatal/Early Infancy Project, and, in the UK, the Sure Start programme.

The High/Scope Perry Preschool Project, which began in the 1960s, was a high-quality, 'head start', pre-school intervention using a participatory learning approach supplemented by weekly home visits. In one of the associated research studies to evaluate outcomes, 123 African Americans born in poverty and considered to be at high risk of failing in school, at the ages of 3 and 4 were randomly assigned to this intervention or to a non-intervention comparison group. A follow-up study 35 years later found that the Perry Preschool participants had had significantly fewer arrests for violent and other crimes than counterparts who had been randomly assigned to a non-treatment group, and that they had higher earnings, and were more likely to hold a job (Schweinhart et al, 2005).

Sure Start is the nearest equivalent in England and Wales to the Perry Preschool Project. Initially set up only in disadvantaged localities, it aims to provide families with children under age 5 with seamless education, health, support and information services from multidisciplinary teams of professionals. There are over 500 local programmes in operation in disadvantaged areas, and many areas have Sure Start children's centres, which build on these local programmes. This programme is at an early stage, having only commenced in 1999, and the impact so far has been mixed. A recent evaluation study found that progress has been made in developing the integrated family support services that had been envisaged and that programmes were 'providing a range of preventative, non-stigmatising services and were making efforts to engage "hard to reach" and minority ethnic families in their areas' (Carpenter et al, 2005: 2). However, referrals to social services had not increased, which might reasonably have been anticipated if there had been success in reaching the most disadvantaged and excluded families. Other reports indicate that parents find such referrals helpful and that children's language skills are being positively affected (DfES, 2005).

Another early intervention programme that has captured wide attention because of its positive outcomes is the Olds's Prenatal/Early Infancy Project, a nurse visitation programme in the US, with associated follow-up research involving three cohorts of parents (Olds, 2006). Four hundred 'European American, rural' expectant mothers were randomly assigned to intervention or control groups. The preventive intervention, involving home visits by nurses, began during the prenatal period and extended through the child's first two years, focusing on the reduction of adverse maternal behaviours during pregnancy (including smoking, alcohol and drug use) and promoting positive parenting skills and healthy lifestyle choices. Because a randomised control design was used, more confidence can be placed in the different outcomes found for these children by the time they reached the age of 15. Among other benefits, the intervention group had significantly fewer arrests and convictions than those in the control group.

Overall, positive outcomes have been obtained from such pre-school programmes in promoting children's cognitive and social-emotional functioning and in reducing rates of child maltreatment (Nelson et al, 2003; Shaw and Gross, 2006). Larger effects have been obtained when there is an educational component that directly involves the children, when the interventions are more intense and longer lasting, and when the families are from impoverished, minority ethnic backgrounds (Nelson et al, 2003).

Experts agree that interventions to prevent mental health problems and associated harmful behaviours are better if applied early. The transforming potential of interventions is more powerful before behaviour patterns such as 'oppositional defiant disorder' become ingrained, and, if optimally timed, may prevent them from developing in the first place (Coid, 2003: 52). While there is a gathering consensus supporting the value of early intervention, at the same time, there is shared recognition that we need more research. As yet, there is insufficient scientific evidence on which to base policies and practices (Harrington and Bailey, 2003).

Ethical and practical issues

When we consider the practicalities of such interventions and the possible uses and abuses of these research data, several questions compete for our attention. Is it morally wrong, stigmatising and scientifically flawed to label anyone – let alone babies – as at high risk of doing harm? Can serious criminality ever be predicted, or the likelihood of it accurately foreseen? What are the consequences of getting it wrong? Should the positive benefits of interventions for families be made selectively or universally available? The moral and practical aspects of these questions are overlapping but, in the space available, aspects of them can be considered under the headings of: genetic determinism; targeting, labelling and stigma; predictive accuracy; and the purpose of interventions.

Genetic determinism

Research on the genetic basis of violence is particularly likely to incur the wrath of those who regard early interventionism as stigmatising and discriminatory. As noted by others (for example, Ellis, 1996; Rose, 2006), contemporary criminological literature gives emphasis to a sociological model of crime, while biological and psychological theories have become unpopular. Academics and civil libertarians tend to be deeply wary of research investigating biogenetic aspects of behaviour, regarding it as retrograde and politically dangerous. For example, not so long ago, a US conference on the genetic roots of violence was cancelled in response to widespread moral objections and the researchers denounced for fostering racial prejudice and promoting a modern-day version of eugenics. Even the messengers are likely to come under attack. When David Rose more recently gave a paper including an account of the research by Moffitt and colleagues, 'the response was viscerally critical. Speakers claimed that it was 'deterministic,' and would surely lead to a wanton attack on civil liberties' (2006: 30). Repugnance for such research is understandable, given the slippery slope from claims to have identified genetic causes of crime to politically motivated branding of certain groups as biologically inferior, as well as a *Minority Report* type of scenario in which people are punished for crimes they have not committed on the basis that they are genetically wired to do so in the future.

Before censuring such research, however, it is important to be clear that researchers in this field, rather than promulgating a deterministic model of behaviour, emphasise that genetic sources of influence on behaviour are *moderated by experiences* (Moffitt, 2005; Rutter et al, 2006). In contrast to an earlier period in research on the origins of psychopathology and conduct disorders, work since the early 1990s has established that 'genetic effects were crucially dependent on gene expression and that such expression was influenced by a wide range of factors, including environmental features' (Rutter et al, 2006: 228). Unfortunately, misleading impressions are fostered by the language that tends to be used when discussing such research. Rather than there being 'genes for' specific types of behaviour, there are indirect genetic effects on the propensity towards some behaviours, and the process is influenced by a diverse range of other factors. The latest wave of behavioural genetics research is multidisciplinary research and 'is working hard to integrate with the wider research agenda on abnormal behaviors and is expanding the agenda to embrace gene-environment interplay' (Moffitt, 2005:

549). Randomised intervention trials that explore gene–environment interplay are planned or under way. This integration of prevention research and behavioural-genetic research, as well as testing etiological theories, aims to investigate the potential role of interventions in preventing the expression of genetic risk, thereby to explore 'just how powerful' the environment can be 'when it is under deliberate control' (Moffitt, 2005: 549). This programme of work, however, is still at an early stage.

Targeting, labelling and stigma

A major ethical question to confront, in considering the implications of such research, is whether to single out children for interventions on the basis that they are considered to be at future risk of serious/persistent involvement in crime, or whether it is only acceptable to make interventions available to the population in general. There is a tension between, on the one hand, arguments for cost-effectiveness of selectively targeting those who will most benefit, and, on the other hand, the inclusiveness of a population (or primary) approach that gives all families with pre-school-age children access to the advantages that such services might bring.

A compromise approach is to target not individual families, but deprived neighbourhoods or groups of children who have come to attention in some way. This avoids labelling individuals, which might stigmatise them and thereby prove self-fulfilling. It could merely extend the labelling effect, though, if it results in the whole neighbourhood or group being stereotyped as a 'problem', with consequent discrimination, perhaps leading to insularity (McCarthy et al, 2004).

In addition to being cost-effective, another strong argument in favour of selective targeting – or a 'high-risk strategy' (Coid, 2003) – is its implications for criminal justice policies aimed at adolescents. This was the argument of Smith, based on findings in the longitudinal Edinburgh Study of Youth in Transition:

> If, as Moffitt argues, the causes of offending are distinctive among those who will continue to offend throughout their lives, and if they are manifest from an early age, then it is inevitable that these individuals will come into contact with a variety of agencies, including social services and the juvenile and adult criminal justice system. This argues that the system should focus its efforts on trying as far as possible to change this relatively small group. Widening the scope of intervention to include many adolescence-limited offenders will dilute the effectiveness of efforts to help the core group of life-course persistent offenders. The pay-off from targeting the core group will be much greater, because they offend more seriously, more frequently and over a longer period of their lives. (Smith, 2005: 193)

Such selective targeting involves a bifurcated policy founded on a dual taxonomy with which not everyone agrees. There are ethical as well as theoretical implications that follow from divisions of people according to classifications of crimes and antisocial behaviour. Many favour a more general theory of criminal involvement that explains variation as a matter of degree along a continuum, while other taxonomies reflect greater heterogeneity of offending patterns based on different causes and different types of crime. To distinguish one group as qualitatively 'different' (as does Moffitt's theory) is potentially very stigmatising. And if it is a label imposed from early life, the consequences might be irreversible. There is a natural abhorrence against the idea of singling out anyone, especially an infant and, even more so, an unborn child, for a negative attribution before they have done anything to deserve it. Also, the effect on parents must be considered. As Coid puts it: 'How will a family react when informed that their 10-year-old son has a 1 in 3 chance of becoming a psychopath in adulthood?' (2003: 54). Used wrongly, there is the prospect that early risk assessments could provide ammunition for racism, sexism and regional inequalities exacerbating the difficulties of already disadvantaged groups (McCarthy et al, 2004).

Given a principled and strength-based approach, however, derogatory labelling can be proscribed and, instead of 'separate' treatment, individuals reached in the spirit of inclusion. Moreover, if very early preventive approaches are successful, then later labelling and criminalisation processes will be foreclosed. A constructive implication of Smith's argument (quoted above), though, is that youth justice policy might revert to former diversionary policies in the case of so-called 'adolescent-limited offenders', while concentrating resources on very early interventions for those at risk of joining that 'high-risk' minority: the alleged 5%–6% who commit 50%–60% of crimes, or, more accurately, criminal convictions. The latter qualification is, of course, a critical one, given the well-known 'justice gap' between all the crimes committed and the small percentage that lead to a conviction. As argued powerfully by Garside, the assumption that most crime is committed by a tiny minority is unsafe but has become 'a matter of received truth' based on 'sexed-up' evidence (2004: 17). However, the need for much more focus on those types of crime that are undercounted by the British Crime Survey (including sexual assault, benefit fraud, white-collar and corporate crime and environmental crime), and the high attrition rate in achieving convictions, do not obviate the value of early interventions that might prevent violence and persistent long-term harm, including self-harm, being perpetrated by the small percentage that *are known* to services. Even if we worry less about their 'volume' crime, the same core group also commit more serious crimes (Shaw and Gross, 2006). Furthermore, maybe the proportion of unconvicted young people is not as great as the justice gap might indicate. As Garside (2004: 9) allows, 'Many people convicted by the courts will inevitably have committed other offences for which they will never be found guilty'.

A prior requisite for selective targeting, of course, is 'greater accuracy in identification of those most likely to become high-rate offenders than is currently possible' (Coid, 2003: 36). Equally important are support and guidance for practitioners in dealing with the inherent tensions and dilemmas they may face in carrying out assessments and screening. Carrying out assessments on future risk is a particularly sensitive area of practice, requiring a principled approach and clear ethical codes (McCarthy et al, 2004).

Predictive accuracy

To a considerable extent, the ethical and moral implications of early risk prediction and targeting hinge on the question of accuracy. Does the research on risk factors and the assessment tools to which they have given rise provide a level of predictive accuracy on which we can rely? The short answer is 'no'. Given their hit-and-miss rate, if selection were for interventions that encroach on liberty and opportunities, then it would be ethically indefensible to use early assessment tools to identify infants as 'high risk'. Although there is agreement that assessment tools (for example, Asset and Risk of Serious Harm – ROSH) are superior to clinical judgements alone, they are not prediction instruments (see Baker, Chapter 2 in this volume); nor is there a blueprint for predicting serious harm.

While some predictions may be accurate, two types of error are possible: errors of under-prediction, or 'false-negatives', where individuals are *not* predicted to be at risk of the behaviour in question but who then *do* engage in it during the follow-up period; and errors of over-prediction, or 'false-positives', where individuals *are* predicted to be at risk of the behaviour in question but then *do not* engage in it during the follow-up period. The baseline cut-off points will affect which type of error is most likely. In the case of early assessments that infants are at high risk of future serious offending, the likelihood of errors seems high because of the subjectivity involved in deciding on critical factors like 'troublesomeness' and 'poor parenting'.

Analysts conclude that: 'Our ability to predict rare behaviors such as violence – even in samples exhibiting higher-than-average rates of violence – is severely limited. False-positive rates of 50% or greater are common in all schemes that seek to predict violent or dangerous behavior in individuals' (Auerhahn, 2006: 777). In the Dunedin Study, early indicators of antisocial behaviour enabled prediction of 70% of the cases with conduct disorder problems at the age of 11, but at the cost of a high false-positive rate (White et al, 1990). One recent review of the association between pre-school indicators and criminal convictions found that the proportion of cases predicted to be at risk of committing an offence and those that actually did so was 19%, while 'only just half of the cases having a later criminal conviction would be identified' (Stevenson and Goodman, 2001: 201). A study to identify early predictors of violence and homicide by young men, using data from the Pittsburgh Youth Study, developed a model that correctly identified 76% of cases and controls, but it cautioned that the relatively high false-error rate prohibited the use of predictive screening devices. In numerous cases, the risk factors for violence were not observed before adolescence and the associated factors appeared gradually over the years, thus indicating that long-term factors need to be tackled as well as early childhood factors (Loeber et al, 2005).

The significance of such errors depends on the purpose and consequences of prediction. The due process concerns are minimised, for example, if a false-positive assessment leads to social benefits rather than restrictions on liberty, and if a false-negative assessment does not place anyone in jeopardy or result in a child being denied interventions that he/she needs. However, a high rate of false-positives has resource implications if interventions are used inappropriately and will undermine confidence in assessment procedures, as well as the principles of evidence-based practice (Dal Pra, 2006). Perhaps we can hold out hope that further research will advance our understanding of the mechanisms that lead to harmful behaviour, and that such models can be drawn on to bring in more contributory factors that will increase the accuracy of assessment tools (Coid, 2003). On the other hand, the prospect of adding genetic factors to prediction tools is alarming, given the inordinate faith placed by courts in 'scientific evidence' and the miscarriages of justice that have ensued (Beecher-Monas and Garcia-Rill, 2006).

The purpose of interventions

So much depends on the nature of interventions and what those attending stand to gain or lose. If screening for 'high risk of serious harm' resulted in, for example, placement into cryogenic stasis (the fate of individuals in *Minority Report*), then an accurate prediction tool would not make that outcome any the more acceptable. The idea of labelling a unborn child as having a genetic propensity towards violence, watching over the pregnancy and then referring mother and baby to a specialist centre for people who are different, conjures images of state interference of Orwellian proportions. But access to nurseries, health care and 'head start' education hardly sound sinister or punitive in intent. Applying Farrington's straightforward logic, if preventive treatment had been applied to all of those boys in the Cambridge Study who were identifiable before the event as 'at risk' of early-onset offending, then 'the one-quarter who were "false-positives" would have been treated unnecessarily. However, if the treatment consisted of extra benefits to families, and if it was effective in reducing the offending of the other three-quarters, the benefits might outweigh the costs and early identification might be justifiable' (2003: 23).

A balanced appraisal should return to the theoretical underpinning of the research basis of early interventions. The case for early targeting that emerges from this body of research is that disordered behaviour is more malleable or preventable in the early years but is cumulative if neglected and becomes entrenched as a result of socio-environmental interactions. As Moffitt makes clear in her now-classic paper, left unaided, there is a 'pernicious' continuity in the behaviour patterns that have their earliest manifestations in infancy. If no attempt is made to protect the health of prenatal and neonatal infants, and if young children miss out on opportunities to arrest or reverse the kinds of neuropsychological difficulties and abusive treatment that are so implicated in the development of serious problems, then a vital stage for averting this cumulative process is missed, and 'the child who "steps off on the wrong foot" remains on an ill-starred path' (1993: 682). This theory of cumulative continuity is empirically supported by longitudinal studies, at least during the first half of the life course (Moffitt et al, 2002).

The future of early developmental prevention

In the light of the preceding outline of research, interventions and their implications, should early developmental prevention be condemned or welcomed? While the research base remains a 'work in progress', experts in this field of study advocate the expansion of early intervention schemes:

> The good news is that many programs are effective in preventing future offending. My conclusion is that early interventions, which target children under age 12, are particularly needed.... It is surely better to intervene early in criminal careers rather than to wait until numerous people have been victimized. Hence, early identification and preventive intervention seems likely to be an effective strategy to prevent crime. As with public health, prevention is better than cure. (Farrington, 2005: 244)

Based on progress in this field of research, Farrington and colleagues propose that the UK should follow the example of other countries, including Sweden and Canada, which have set up a separate national agency to prevent crime and antisocial behaviour. Their vision is for a national prevention agency that would have a mandate for primary prevention of crime, would provide training in prevention science, funding and guidance for implementing local prevention programmes, and an agenda for research and practice. They see the Sure Start programme and the Every Child Matters strategy as a basis for the development of a rigorously evaluated, large-scale evidence-based integrated national strategy for the reduction of crime and associated social problems (Farrington and Coid, 2003; Farrington, 2005).

To some extent, their vision is now being realised. The Reaching Out strategy proposed by the Social Exclusion Task Force (Cabinet Office, 2006) is another move in the shift from a treatment approach to a prevention approach. It sets out plans for a nurse visiting scheme, which is clearly influenced by the Olds's Prenatal/Early Infancy Project (Olds et al, 1998), and pilots to test approaches for tackling conduct disorders in childhood. The Sure Start programme is being reconfigured from a range of local initiatives into a mainstream service, with children's centres set up in every community, but with a greater investment in deprived areas (DfES, 2005). The target is to create 3,500 such centres by 2010. The disappointing record so far in reaching those families whom Sure Start was most intended to support has been acknowledged (DfES, 2005; Cabinet Office, 2006) and the stated policy now is to place more emphasis on outreach and home visiting, and to monitor trends in usage and to tailor services according to local needs and characteristics of the area (DfES, 2005).

In the present climate of suspicion about the encroachments of a preventive state (Zedner, 2007), perhaps we do not welcome such developments as much as they deserve. As Farrington (2005: 8) notes, 'the social costs of incorrect predictions seem likely to be rated higher than the social benefits of correct predictions'. This is an argument for assessment tools with baselines that err on the side of 'false-negatives', but when it comes to programmes that enlarge the opportunities of those receiving them, and may help them to escape a pernicious trap (Moffitt, 1993), maybe the benefits should be weighted more highly.

It remains to be seen whether recent policy favouring pre-crime preventive measures will be accompanied by the rigorous and independent evaluations that such initiatives need. More research is needed on several fronts. A long period of time is necessary in which to determine the success of risk assessment instruments and to develop them so that they are more reliable and sensitive to critical variables (Farrington and Coid, 2003). And further longitudinal research is needed that begins in early childhood and is focused on high risk of serious harm (Shaw and Gross, 2006). We need more randomised experiments to evaluate the effectiveness of interventions, and more systematic reviews and meta-analyses, as well as cost–benefit analyses (Farrington, 2005). Not least, there is concurrence among investigators that 'the study of antisocial behavior is [still] stuck in the 'risk factor'' stage' (Moffitt, 2005: 533) and that the main gap is for further research into causal factors.

Conclusion

'It's never too early' is the title of a chapter in a recent book reviewing research and evidence-based practice in early intervention (Farrington and Welsh, 2006). In keeping with this sentiment, one distinguished reviewer of the book wrote: 'The current willingness to allow at-risk children to develop unimpeded into serious, chronic offenders represents an inexcusable policy failure and threat to public safety' (Cullen, 2006). The present British government appears to have taken such advice to heart.

This chapter aimed to consider some of the research and intervention experiments on which recent policy shifts are based – and to do so without prejudice given the controversies and moral issues to which they give rise. While the research base is voluminous, many questions nevertheless remain unanswered in the absence of further large-scale and long-term research. This is particularly the case if we believe there is merit in distinguishing adaptive offending behaviour from antisocial behaviour that is symptomatic of lifelong difficulties, and in focusing resources and services on a minority identified as at risk of joining the latter group. In a society obsessed with risk, including crime before it has happened, it is not outlandish to speculate on the prospect of infants being locked up for future transgressions on the basis of prediction. But is the government's pre-birth 'reaching out' policy of the same order? In a focus on the offspring of 'the excluded of the excluded, the deeply excluded' (Blair, 2006) who may not want or know how to access 'universal services' but nevertheless stand to benefit most from them, should we be wary and full of censure? The objectives and outcomes of such programmes and the way people are treated as recipients of them are surely what matters. Before we condemn such an approach, it behoves us to at least be in touch with the practice of such interventions, the types of services provided, and the motivations of those who work with the target families and who are trying to reach them.

References

Auerhahn, K. (2006) 'Conceptual and methodological issues in the prediction of dangerous behavior', *Criminology and Public Policy*, vol 5, no 4, pp 771–8.

Beecher-Monas, E. and Garcia-Rill, E. (2006) 'Genetic predictions of future dangerousness: Is there a blueprint for violence?', *Law and Contemporary Problems*, vol 69, no 1–2, pp 301–42.

Blair, T. (2006) 'Our nation's future – Social exclusion', paper to seminar on social exclusion, held at 10 Downing Street, 5 September (www.number-10.gov.uk/output/page10037.asp).

Cabinet Office (2006) *Reaching out: An action plan on social exclusion*, London: COI.

Carpenter, J., Griffin, M. and Brown, S. (2005) *The impact of Sure Start on social services*, Research Report SSU/2005/FR/015, Nottingham: DfES Publications.

Caspi, A., McClay, J., Moffitt, T.E., Mill, J., Martin, J., Craig, I.W., Taylor, A. and Poulton, R. (2002) 'Role of genotype in the cycle of violence in maltreated children', *Science*, vol 297, pp 851–4.

Coid, J.W. (2003) 'Formulating strategies for the primary prevention of adult antisocial behaviour: "High-risk" or "population" strategies?', in D.P. Farrington and J.W. Coid (eds), *Early prevention of adult antisocial behaviour*, Cambridge: Cambridge University Press, pp 32-78.

Cullen, F. (2006) review of D.P Farrington and B.C. Welsh, *Saving children from a life of crime: Early risk factors and effective interventions*, Oxford: Oxford University Press (www.oup.com/uk/catalogue/?ci=9780195304091).

Dal Pra, Z. (2006) '"Community corrections": Quest to predict violence', *Criminology and Public Policy*, vol 5, no 4, pp 779–84.

DfES (2005) 'Sure Start Children's Centres: Practice guidance' (available at www.surestart.gov.uk/improvingquality/guidance/practiceguidance/).

Ellis, L. (1996) 'A discipline in peril: Sociology's future hinges on curing its biophobia', *American Sociologist*, vol 27, pp 21–41.

Farrington, D.P. (2000) 'Explaining and preventing crime: The globalization of knowledge', *Criminology*, vol 38, no 1, pp 1–24.

Farrington, D.P. (2005) 'Early identification and preventive intervention: How effective is this strategy?', *Criminology and Public Policy*, vol 4, no 2, pp 237–48.

Farrington, D.P. and Coid, J.W. (2003) 'Conclusions and the way forward', in D.P. Farrington and J.W. Coid (eds), *Early prevention of adult antisocial behaviour*, Cambridge: Cambridge University Press, pp 356-68

Farrington, D.P. and Welsh, B.C. (2006) *Saving children from a life of crime: Early risk factors and effective interventions*, Oxford: Oxford University Press.

Garside, R. (2004) *Crime, persistent offenders and the justice gap*, Discussion Paper no 1, London: Crime and Society Foundation.

Haapasalo, J. and Pokela, E. (1998) 'Child rearing and child abuse antecedents of criminality', *Aggression and Violent Behaviour*, vol 4, no 1, pp 107–27.

Harrington, R. and Bailey, S. (2003) *The scope for preventing antisocial personality disorder by intervening in adolescence*, Liverpool: NHS National Programme on Forensic Mental Health Research and Development.

Loeber, R., Pardini, D., Homish, D.L., Wei, E.H., Crawford, A.M., Farrington, D., Stouthamer-Loeber, M., Creemers, J., Koehler, S.A. and Rosenfeld, R. (2005) 'The prediction of violence and homicide in young men', *Journal of Consulting and Clinical Psychology*, vol 73, no 6, pp 1074–88.

McCarthy, P., Laing, K. and Walker, J. (2004) *Offenders of the future? Assessing the risk of children and young people becoming involved in criminal or antisocial behaviour*, Research Report RR545, London: Department for Education and Skills.

Moffitt, T.E. (1993). 'Adolescence-limited and life-course-persistent antisocial behavior: A developmental taxonomy', *Psychological Review*, vol 100, no 4, pp 674–701.

Moffitt, T.E. (2005) 'The new look of behavioral genetics in developmental psychopathology: Gene-environment interplay in antisocial behaviors', *Psychological Bulletin*, vol 131, no 4, pp 533–54.

Moffitt, T.E., Caspi, A., Harrington, H. and Milne, B.J. (2002) 'Males on the life-course-persistent and adolescence-limited antisocial pathways: Follow-up at age 26 years', *Development and Psychopathology*, vol 14, pp 179–207.

Nelson, G., Westhues, A. and MacLeod, J. (2003) 'A meta-analysis of longitudinal research on preschool prevention programs for children', *Prevention and Treatment*, vol 6, December, pp 1–67.

Olds, D (2006). 'The nurse–family partnership: An evidence based preventive intervention', *Infant Mental Health Journal*, vol 27, no 1, pp 5–25.

Olds, D., Pettitt, L.M., Robinson, J., Henderson, C., Eckenrode, J., Kitzman, H., Cole, B. and Powers, J. (1998) 'Reducing risks for antisocial behavior with a program of prenatal and early childhood home visits', *Journal of Community Psychology*, vol 26, no 1, pp 65–83.

Rose, D. (2006) 'Lives of crime', *Prospect*, 125, August 2006 (available at www.propect-magazine.co.uk/pdfarticle).

Rutter, M., Moffitt, T.E. and Caspi, A. (2006) 'Gene–environment interplay and psychopathology: Multiple varieties but real effects', *Journal of Child Psychology and Psychiatry*, vol 47, no 3/4, pp 226–61.

Sampson, R.J., Morenoff, J.D. and Gannon-Rowley, T. (2002) 'Assessing "neighborhood effects": Social processes and new directions in research', *Annual Review of Sociology*, vol 28, pp 443–78.

Schweinhart, L.J., Montie, J., Xiang, Z., Barnett, W.S., Belfield, C.R. and Nores, M. (2005) *Lifetime effects: The High/Scope Perry Preschool study through age 40*, Monographs of the High/Scope Educational Research Foundation no 14, Ypsilanti, MI: High/Scope Press.

Shaw, D.S. and Gross, H.E. (2006) 'Early childhood and the development of delinquency: What have we learned from recent longitudinal research', report for the National Institute of Justice (available at www.pitt.edu/~momchild/publications_contents.htm).

Smith, D.J. (2005) 'The effectiveness of the juvenile justice system', *Criminal Justice*, vol 5, no 2, pp 181–95.

Stevenson, J. and Goodman, R. (2001) 'Association between behaviour at age 3 years and adult criminality', *British Journal of Psychiatry*, vol 179, no 3, pp 197–202.

Wikström, P-O.H. and Butterworth, D.A. (2006) *Adolescent crime: Individual differences and lifestyles*, Cullompton: Willan.

White, J., Moffitt, T.E., Earls, F., Robins, L.N. and Silva, P.A. (1990) 'How early can we tell? Preschool predictors of boys' conduct disorder and delinquency', *Criminology*, vol 28, no 4, pp 507–33.

Zedner, L. (2007) 'Pre-crime and post-criminology?', *Theoretical Criminology*, special issue on 'Criminology, Public Policy and Public Intellectuals', vol 11, no 2, pp 261-81.

Conclusions

Rob Allen

The contributions to this volume raise important policy questions in respect of three overlapping areas: the prevention of serious violent crime by early intervention with children at risk; the assessment of young people once they are in the criminal justice system; and the management and treatment of young offenders in the community and in institutions.

Early intervention

As far as prevention is concerned, one main dilemma is the extent to which it is possible or desirable to target children for an intervention at an early stage in their lives, before they have committed a crime. Ros Burnett speculates on the prospect of infants being locked up for future crimes on the basis of prediction, setting this against the increasingly prevalent view that 'the current willingness to allow at-risk children to develop unimpeded into serious chronic offenders represents an inexcusable policy failure and threat to public safety' (Cullen, 2006). In 2006 Tony Blair argued that:

> Where it is clear, as it very often is, at young age, that children are at risk of being brought up in a dysfunctional home where there are multiple problems, say of drug abuse or offending, then instead of waiting until the child goes off the rails, we should act early enough, with the right help, support and disciplined framework for the family, to prevent it. (Blair, 2006b)

He went on to claim that 'you can detect and predict the children and families likely to go wrong' and that:

> There has been great progress in our ability to spot the risk factors associated with subsequent anti-social behaviour. Of course prediction will never be perfect. But the combination of risk and protection means that we can now be reasonably confident that we can identify likely problems at a very early stage.

Burnett (Chapter 7: 106, this volume) offers a more measured view about prediction: 'Does the research on risk factors and the assessment tools to which they have given rise provide a level of predictive accuracy on which we can rely? The short answer is "no".' Tools, it seems, do not predict all those who will go on to commit crime and they identify some who will not.

In practice, this may not matter if the result of identification is social benefits. As Blair (2006b) puts it 'this is not stigmatising the child or the family. It may be the only way to save them and the wider community from the consequences of inaction'. He admits that

> Intervention can sound very sinister. Actually, in the great bulk of cases it means that extra help and support can be provided. It might mean that a more intense health visitor programme is arranged. Or it might mean parenting classes are offered; or help with drug or alcohol abuse. Or placing families within projects like the Dundee project where the family is given help but within a proper, disciplined framework. (Blair, 2006b)

While these examples of interventions certainly sound like 'social benefits', there are still potential causes for concern. The first relates to the now unfashionable labelling theory, which holds that people officially labelled as criminals tend to adopt a criminal identity and find it very hard to escape from it subsequently. This can result from a combination of how people see themselves and how others, particularly state agencies, see them and treat them. While such effects may be less acute in respect of 'at risk' rather than 'criminal' labels, whatever the positive intentions of targeting and intervention, unintended consequences cannot be ruled out. As Hazel Kemshall says in her chapter, 'early prevention is targeted at "needs" but justified on the basis of preventing future risks, and most particularly the risk of crime' (Chapter 1: 10, this volume).

Second, while Tony Blair (2006a) made it clear that this is not about 'blaming' anyone for what has happened, it is, he said, about 'coupling social rights with social responsibilities'. While 'labelling-free' help and support may indeed be provided in the great bulk of cases, this leaves the door open for more 'sinister' interventions with the minority. Reductions in child or housing benefit have been among the measures canvassed by this government for recalcitrant families. In his criminal justice speech in 2006, Blair suggested far earlier intervention with some of these families before they offend 'and certainly before they want such intervention' (Blair, 2006a). As Mike Nash suggests (citing Blair in Muncie, 2006), 'ever-earlier intervention is justified as a pre-emptive strike and, as a consequence, failure to 'take advantage' may result in stiffer penalties later on'.

A sensible way forward that does not throw out the early intervention baby with the targetting bathwater might simply be to expand the availability of service provision for those children and their families who have already come to the attention of the authorities. Burnett quotes David Smith's argument (Smith, 2005: 193) that if 'the causes of offending are distinctive among those who will continue to offend throughout their lives ... then it is inevitable that these individuals will come into contact with a variety of agencies, including social services'. If, as Blair (2006a) puts it, 'the vast majority offered help, take it' the answer would seem to lie in offering more help: a larger quantity and wider variety of measures designed to encourage affectionate families, adequate attention from parents, educational achievement, and so on.

Rather than targeting propensity to commit crime, better services could be provided on the basis of vulnerability and existing involvement with agencies. Candidates for voluntary intervention could include the 570,000 children who are referred to social services for child maltreatment, the 125,000 children whose parents are in prison, the 60,000 children in care and 40,000 born to teenage parents as well as children under the age of criminal responsibility who are involved in delinquency. Skilled, accessible help and support to these groups should be provided under the aegis of properly funded children's services that integrate the prevention of crime alongside the essential outcomes for children pursued by the Every Child Matters agenda. A wide range of preventive programmes needs to be developed, including, for example, much wider use of functional family therapy as is the case in Sweden. Such an approach would have the advantage of seeking to prevent offending, harm and vulnerability among young people rather than simply focusing on crime (see Allen, forthcoming).

Assessment of risk of serious harm

Many of the caveats about prediction discussed above apply more widely to the process of assessment, but some of the key dilemmas relate specifically to the assessment of youngsters' risk of serious harm to others. Is it possible to place a risk approach at the centre of Youth Offending Team (YOT) practice without losing a focus on meeting needs and respecting the rights of children and young people? Does the control of the risk posed by small numbers displace more welfare-based approaches to *all* offenders or lead to a general improvement in analysis and decision-making skills? The evidence does suggest that improvements are needed in the quality of assessments of risks. Asset completion is of mixed quality, with one in five not sufficient (more in cases of violence). Yet it may be the very risk 'factorology' approach that is alienating some practitioners: 'The coverage of the tools, and often their emphasis upon risk, prevention and control, has affected the commitment of workers to their use' (Kemshall, Chapter 1: 10, this volume).

Three ways forward suggest themselves. First is the development of an approach that better values and enhances the professional skills involved in undertaking assessments, keeping in balance the importance of procedural compliance with 'appropriate levels of understanding, knowledge and ability to work with challenging and often highly troubled young people' (Baker, Chapter 2: 34, this volume). There should be more specific training and awareness-raising for YOT staff around the issues of child protection and child abuse that covers the impact of maltreatment on behaviour.

Second is to heighten the focus in assessment on dynamic factors 'that can be changed by interventions' and include 'data on protective factors and strengths' (Bailey et al, Chapter 4: 58, this volume). After all, the main purpose of assessment is to establish how risk can be mitigated through an appropriate programme of work. On the basis of Gwyneth Boswell's work, there seems a strong case too for giving a greater prominence to child maltreatment as a primary predisposing risk factor in likely subsequent offending in the Youth Justice Board (YJB) risk factors. Wherever a child is charged or convicted of a serious violent or sexual crime, referral could be made to the local child protection service for child protection core assessment. The threshold of seriousness might be that the child is charged with an offence under section 90/91 of the 2000 Powers of Criminal Courts (Sentencing) Act or sentenced to detention for public protection (section 226 of the 2003 Criminal Justice Act).

Finally, much greater attention needs to be paid to what the young people themselves make of the difficulties they are in and how to resolve them. Given the commitment that, in planning services and interventions, children should be consulted and their voices should be carefully listened to and taken into consideration, it is troubling that in Baker's sample of Risk of Serious Harm (ROSH) assessments, 'no reference was made to the young person's self-assessment form … in any of the ROSH forms or the staff interviews' (Baker, Chapter 2: 29, this volume).

It seems likely that an in-depth understanding of young people's needs, wishes and aspirations is more likely to enable programmes to be developed that help youngsters embark on a journey to desistance than would a narrow focus on the risks they present and the deficits they suffer.

Such an approach would need to tackle the problem of transition to adulthood and how the current configuration of services allows for youngsters to fall through the gap at 18; too old for the YOT but still emotionally and behaviourally in need of educational, health and social care responses. A thorough developmental approach to young people could recast assessment as a stimulus to a range of imaginative therapeutic programmes that are essential to long-term reductions of risk.

Management

The final set of questions relate to what we should actually do with young people who offend seriously and pose a risk of further harm. A recent report by this author suggested that the current responses to the most damaged children who present the greatest needs and highest risks are inadequate and can make matters worse (Allen, 2006). We need, it argued, a wider range of community-based and residential placements for young people who cannot stay with their families, with a change in the law to permit children sentenced to detention and training orders to be placed in non-custodial institutions and, in particular, therapeutic establishments.

The chapters in this volume set out the range of activities in which further investment and service delivery improvements are needed. Perhaps unfortunately, under the heading 'risk management tactics', Kemshall lists 'stable and suitable accommodation; positive involvement of parents, carers and mentors; specific therapies …; addressing drug, substance and alcohol abuse; constructive use of leisure time; avoidance of antisocial peers; school attendance; employment' (Kemshall, Chapter 1: 15, this volume). Nash quotes the importance attached by desistance studies to stabilising factors in offenders' lives (accommodation, work and relationships). Boswell highlights the importance of addressing earlier life events, particularly abuse, which 'may prove to be more criminogenic than any peer group pressure or substance addiction' (Boswell, Chapter 3: 48, this volume).

On the mental health side, Bailey et al quote the admirable aspiration of standard 9 (the CAMHS standard) of the Children's National Service Framework but, as Maggie Blyth says, children and young people who offend have more health needs than the non-offending population of children and provision remains inadequate, particularly for 16 and 17 year olds who fall between child and adult services. Bailey et al quote a study, finding that only 20% of depressed incarcerated youth and 10% of adolescents with other disorders were receiving treatment.

What can we conclude? First, perhaps, that the most obvious way of protecting the public and reducing risk – incarceration – is costly, ineffective and in some cases counterproductive and brutal. There are aspects of prison and other institutions that can be improved, for example 'proper provision should be made for interventions such as counselling following child abuse and other background traumata' (Boswell, Chapter 3: 48, this volume), but there must be concern about the growing use of indeterminate sentences. The number of 15–21 year olds in prison subject to these sentences almost doubled between January 2006 and January 2007, from 288 to 558 (Home Office, 2007) reflecting the spiralling use for all ages of sentences for public protection. There is a need to ensure not only that the regimes available to these young people produce positive outcomes but also that the Parole Board applies approaches to decisions about release that are appropriate to the distinctive needs of young people.

Second, there are important issues about staff who work with young offenders in whatever setting. Bailey et al are surely right to highlight the skills required to engage a young offender in a therapeutic alliance: 'To engage actively … professionals need to listen attentively and show interest in the young person's perspective' (Bailey et al, Chapter 4: 64, this volume). The quality of relationships with all young people in trouble is particularly important and perhaps underrated. It is even more significant in respect of those whose delinquent and risky behaviour reflects the failures of attachment and bonding in their earlier years. The well-publicised impact of projects like Kids Company in Southwark shows how sustained and unconditional commitment to damaged young people is necessary if they are to be engaged, let alone helped to change.

Third, a properly joined-up set of measures for young people in England can only really be developed under the aegis of a government department responsible for meeting the needs of children. A study of children who present challenging behaviour suggested that, historically, whether the problem child has been cared for, punished, educated or treated has often been a matter of chance, depending upon which individuals in which agency happened to pick up his or her case (Visser, 2003). A more sensible approach is for responses to children to be made on the basis of what best will meet their needs and address risks. The outcomes for children, set out in the 2004 Children Act – being healthy, staying safe, enjoying and achieving, making a contribution and achieving economic well-being – are as appropriate for young offenders as they are other young people. They offer a sensible set of values that should underpin the range of community-based and residential services that are needed for young people in conflict with the law. The shared responsibility for youth justice by the Ministry of Justice and the Department for Children, Schools and Families offers the prospect of better governance in the future.

Conclusion

This kind of balanced approach is sorely needed in a political climate in which Tony Blair saw the need for a change in the culture of political and legal decision making: 'a complete change of mindset, an avowed, articulated determination to make protection of the law-abiding public the priority and to measure that not by the theory of the textbook but by the reality of the street and community in which real people live real lives' (Blair, 2006a). As one of the commentators to Blair's speech, Ian Loader, has replied, 'sustaining a decent, civilized, liberal democratic society requires us not to speak of 'eradication' (the term the PM resorted to when launching the Respect agenda), but of addressing problems in ways that that enable citizens to *live securely with risk*' (Loader, 2006, emphasis in original). There is an urgent need for a more honest conversation that makes the links between the UK's place at the bottom of a league table of child well-being in the EU (Bradshaw et al, 2007) and the problems that are caused by young people; and makes the case for investing in the range of preventive and therapeutic services that can serve to reduce the risks they pose to themselves, victims of crime and the wider community.

References
Allen, R. (forthcoming) 'Early intervention with children at risk: international examples', in R. Loeber, N.W. Slot and P. Van de Laan (eds), *Tomorrow's criminals*, Aldershot: Ashgate.
Allen, R. (2006) *From punishment to problem solving*, London: Centre for Crime and Justice Studies.

Blair, T. (2006a) 'Our nation's future – criminal justice', speech, 23 June 2006 (available at: www.pm.gov.uk/output/Page9728.asp).

Blair, T. (2006b) 'Our nation's future – social exclusion', speech, 5 September 2006 (available at: www.pm.gov.uk/output/Page10037.asp).

Bradshaw, J., Hoelscher, P. and Richardson, D. (2007), 'An index of child well-being in the European Union', *Social Indicators Research*, vol 80, no 1, pp 133–77.

Cullen, F. (2006) review of D.P Farrington and B.C Welsh, *Saving children from a life of crime: Early risk factors and effective interventions*, Oxford: Oxford University Press (www.oup.com/uk/catalogue/?ci=9780195304091).

Home Office (2007) *Population in custody monthly tables: January 2007*, London: Home Office.

Loader, I. (2006) 'Rebalancing the criminal justice system?' (available at: www.pm.gov.uk/output/Page9701.asp).

Smith, D.J. (2005) 'The effectiveness of the juvenile justice system', *Criminal Justice*, vol 5, no 2, pp 181–95.

Visser, J. (2003) *A study of young people with challenging behaviour*, London: Ofsted.